SYMBIOSIS AND SEPARATION

*Towards a Psychology
of Culture*

SYMBIOSIS AND SEPARATION

*Towards a Psychology
of Culture*

Richard A. Koenigsberg

**The Library of Art and Social Science
New York**

Copyright © 1989 by the
Library of Art and Social Science

All rights reserved. No part of this book may be reproduced in any form (except for brief quotations in connection with reviews) without the written permission of the publisher.

LCN: 88-93056
ISBN: 0-915042-20-7

Manufactured in the United States of America

Designed and Computer Typeset by
Dorothy Wasserman Associates, Inc.
New York City

Table of Contents

Chapter	I.	The Dual Nature of the Human Ego	1
Chapter	II.	The Conversion Process as a Response to Separation	9
Chapter	III.	The Denial of Separateness	13
Chapter	IV.	Internalization	19
Chapter	V.	The Struggle for Separateness	25
Chapter	VI.	The Fantasy of Merger as a Source of Anxiety	29
Chapter	VII.	Conflict and Ambivalence Surrounding Separation-Individuation	35
Chapter	VIII.	The Transitional Object and the Struggle to Separate	46
Chapter	IX.	Culture as a Transitional Object	55
Chapter	X.	The Bodily Roots of the Symbol	59
Chapter	XI.	The Bodily Roots of Culture	74
Chapter	XII.	Repression	80
		References	89

CHAPTER I

The Dual Nature of the Human Ego

It would appear that the human ego evolves out of a sense of "oneness" which gradually gives way to the perception of "duality." Thus Margaret Mahler has developed the hypothesis of the "symbiotic phase" as a central feature of human development. Mahler defines symbiosis as

> ...that state of undifferentiation, of fusion with mother, in which the "I" is not yet differentiated from the "not I."
> (1968, p. 9)

She describes the symbiotic phase as follows:

> The essential feature of symbiosis is hallucinatory or delusional, somatopsychic omnipotent fusion with the representation of the mother and, in particular, the delusion of a common boundary of the two actually and physically separate individuals.
> (1968, p. 9)

> From the second month on, dim awareness of the need-satisfying object marks the beginning of the phase of normal symbiosis, in which the infant behaves and functions as though he and his mother were an omnipotent system--a dual unity with one common boundary.
> (1968, p. 9)

The symbiotic phase, then, it would appear, consists of the cognitive experience of "oneness," a sense of narcissistic unity and omnipotence, the central feature of which is the illusion that the *other is a part of the self*. The mother, during the earliest phases of development, gratifies the needs of the child, while the child makes little effort and is not aware that an external object is responsible for the gratification of its needs. The sense of easy, passive gratification possesses a "magical" quality: insofar as the external world has not yet been registered in consciousness as a separate domain of reality, there is a sense that gratification is emanating from *within the domain of the self*.

The mother is actually "out there," existing as a separate entity in the external world. But for the child, during this early period, the mother is experienced to be a part of the self. So the primitive ego experiences itself as "one," even as that which occurs within the domain of the ego is the consequence of the interaction of two persons. The mother is experienced, in a delusional way, to be a part of the self. This is the psychic delusion of symbiosis, the delusion of a "common boundary" which encompasses two separate individuals. This delusion of "two within one" is the "dual-unity" situation.

Given this conception of the symbiotic phase, the evolution of "separation-individuation" is not separation as it is generally conceived, separation as movement away from an object in the external world. Rather, separation within the framework of this concept consists of a gradual loss of self, the dawning awareness that what was originally conceived to be a part of one's ego is not actually a part of one's ego. Thus Mahler states that "the symbiotic phase involves a loss of a part of the ego" (1968, p. 9).

The early experience of "oneness" was, in actuality, an illusion. The gradual recognition that the second individual who constituted the "dual unity" is outside the self rather than inside it contradicts this fantasy. Thus, to abandon the symbiotic fantasy is to lose a part of oneself, that is, to separate from a part of one's ego. Separation-individuation, from this point of view, is the gradual shrinking of the narcissistic ego, the work toward abandoning the sense of omnipotence. It is a gradual "splitting" of the self, such that one's being is to be identified only with the actuality of one's organismic self, and not with that part of the ego (the mother) which was identified with the self, but was not actually a part of the self.

The ultimate goal of the process of separation-individuation is the achievement of a self which is a *unity*, consisting of one's own being. To achieve such a unity, one must abandon the symbiotic fantasy, must "drop" from the ego the "second part of the self" (the mother) which is not actually the self. It means abandoning the sense of power, and the expectation of gratification, which was associated with the fantasy that *there was an object within the ego, other than one's self, which could gratify one's needs.*

We now turn to the work of Edward, Ruskin and Turrini (1981), who explicate and expand upon Mahler's concepts. They discuss the roots of selfhood and the sense of identity as deriving from the body ego:

> Early inner body experiences contribute, ultimately, to the development of the body ego and the body-self, forming the very core of the self. They remain the crystallization point of the "feelings of self" around which a "sense of identity" will become established.
>
> (1981, p. 5)

> Before a mother becomes recognized as a need-satisfying mother, she is experienced coenesthetically.
>
> (1981, p. 5)

The term "coenesthesia" comes from the Greek, "common feeling," and is defined by Webster's dictionary as "the mass of undifferentiated sensations that make one aware of the body and its conditions." The crucial point made by Edward, et al., is that if the ego is "first and foremost a body ego," then the early body-ego contains the illusion of one's mother as a part of one's own ego. The body-ego, in the dual-unity phase, is an ego which reflects the child's experiences of his own body plus the experiences of one's mother's body as connected to one's own body. The body ego is a *mother in child body-ego*.

But let us back-track briefly. Edward, et al., indicate that Mahler distinguished between an early state of autism or "absolute primary narcissism" on the one hand, and a later state of primary narcissism or symbiosis on the other. The difference would appear to be that during the second phase there is a *sensing* of an object outside the self, whereas in the earlier phase there is no such sensing of an external object:

> From the second month on, a dim awareness of the need-gratifying mother appears to take place and marks the beginning of the phase of normal symbiosis in which the infant and mother form a dual unity within a common boundary. Mahler has referred to the beginning phase of symbiosis as a state of primary narcissism (in contrast to the autistic stage of absolute primary narcissism). The distinction is made by virtue of the fact that now the infant appears to be dimly cognizant that need-satisfaction cannot be provided by oneself but comes from somewhere outside.
> (1981, p. 6)

During the early part of symbiosis that merges with the autistic phase, coenesthetic receptivity still operates, and there appears to be an overlapping between the coenesthetic sense of the mother as the "symbiotic half of the self" and the dim awareness of her function as a need-gratifier and, therefore, somewhat "out there."

(1981, p. 6)

What is being suggested by these passages is the following: the autistic phase carries with it no perception of the object as existing as a part of the external world. The mother is experienced, or coenesthetically sensed, as the "symbiotic part of the self," and therefore the fantasy of symbiosis is not required.

The symbiotic phase proper begins only when the infant becomes "dimly cognizant" that need satisfaction is coming from outside the self rather than from within the self. It is at this point that the symbiotic fantasy or hallucination develops, the function of which is to extend or perpetuate the pleasurable illusion of oneness. The function of the symbiotic fantasy is to perpetuate the dream that the mother's body is a part of one's own body.

If the mother is experienced as the "symbiotic half of the self," it is clear, then, that separation-individuation is best conceived, not as the separation of a subject from an object in the external world, but as the severing of a part of oneself from one's self; in separating from the mother, one is simultaneously "lopping off" a part of one's ego. Edward, et al., report:

> There are clients, for instance, who in speaking of the death of a mother...note a feeling in their bodies as if they have lost some vague aspect of the bodily self.
>
> (1981, p. 6)

And Neils Maizels, discussing his clinical data, concludes that "Separation from the mother...is equated with a mutilation of one's own body."

We may hypothesize that the gradual perception that one is separate from the symbiotic half of the self is one of the profound traumas of childhood, and of human life. It is simultaneously to be separated from the delusion that gratification is automatic, and to be separated from the illusion of narcissistic omnipotence. The loss of what was imagined to be a part of oneself means that one becomes a "shrunken" version of what one once imagined oneself to be: one becomes a frail, human individual. Separation from the delusion of symbiosis, I believe, is the meaning of the human being's "loss of paradise." And Edwards, et al., emphasize that there are *two* aspects to this traumatic experience of separateness: on the one hand, the loss of the source of gratification; and, on the other hand, the loss of the sense of "harmony" associated with the state of dual unity:

> Mahler has noted that we can still observe in the adult intense longings for the symbiotic mother--not just the need-satisfying one but the still coenesthetically remembered part of the self, with whom one experienced the harmony of the dual unity state.
> (1981, p. 6)

We may summarize our argument, then, as follows: the original ego, a body ego, originates in proprioceptive stimulation which consists both of stimuli arising from the interior and exterior of one's own body, as well as from sensations arising from contact with the mother's body. Insofar as the mother, however, during this early phase, is not perceived as an external object, stimulation based on contact with the mother is perceived as if emanating from one's own body. In short, the second self which constitutes the other half of the symbiotic bond is not perceived, by the child, as another self. Rather, the self of the mother tends to be experienced as *existing within one's own body*, as a body which is "connected" to one's own body (something along the lines of an unperceived Siamese twin). And this fantasy of "twoness within oneness" is described by the phrase "dual unity."

Separation-individuation is a term for the gradual process whereby the individual comes to realize that what was once imagined to be a part of one's own body exists, in actuality, as an object in the external world. Separation from the mother is thus experienced as a mutilation of the self, as a shrinking of the ego, as the core of the self gradually "splits" from this omnipotent extension of the self. This "shrinkage" of the ego is extremely traumatic, since it implies the perception of one's smallness, frailty and aloneness, as well as the necessity to recognize that gratification, the fulfillment of one's desires, is not magically provided from within but depends upon one's own efforts.

One may theorize broadly that there are two fundamental reaction-tendencies which follow this traumatic perception. On the one hand, separation is not accepted. The ego strives to maintain the illusion of dual-unity, struggles to "recapture" the experience of narcissistic omnipotence. We shall explore the mechanisms of *denial* in detail in this monograph.

On the other hand, there is a struggle toward separation-individuation. This striving may be characterized as the striving to *achieve the unity of the self*, to develop an autonomous ego whose integrity is not ruptured by that which is alien to the self. That is to say: However "close" to the child the mother may be, however intense the illusion of oneness, the mother is, nonetheless, a discrete organism, a "not self." Thus, insofar as there exists an organismic tendency toward narcissistic integrity or wholeness (the biological tendency of the organism to reject that which is "not self"), there is a tendency to "reject" the mother from within the structure of the ego, *to rid the self of that part of the self which is not actually the self.* To reject the mother, as alien to the self, is to begin to abandon the delusion that the mother is contained within the boundaries of one's own ego.

As we shall see, the conflict between these two reaction tendencies constitutes one of the major dilemmas of human existence: a conflict between the wish to maintain the delusion of dual-unity, on the one hand, with all of the comfort and security that such a delusion seems to provide; and the wish to reject this delusion, on the other, to evolve a unified, "purified" ego, free from forces which would damage its organic integrity.

Chapter II

The Conversion Process as a Response to Separation

I am going to quote extensively in this monograph from a paper by Felix Deutsch, "Symbolization as a Formative Stage in the Conversion Process," which appeared in a collection of papers which he edited, *On the Mysterious Leap from the Mind to the Body: A Study on the Theory of Conversion* (1959). Many of the themes which we are developing here were suggested in this early, important paper. Deutsch is considering the impact of *loss* upon the child's psychic structure, and, more specifically, the tendency toward *conversion* which develops as a response to loss. According to Deutsch:

> The child soon discovers that what he once felt as a part of himself is temporarily or permanently lost. This first awareness of a loss is the origin of a fantasy or illusion, because what is no longer in the realm of, or attached to, the body has disappeared and now belongs to another reality, so to speak. The child reacts to this loss of an object with the attempt to regain it, to retrieve this part of himself, by imagining it. Attempts of this nature continue throughout life and can be considered as the origin of the conversion process.
>
> (1959, pp. 75-76)

This interpretation closely resembles the theory of symbiosis and separation-individuation which we have presented above. The first experience of separation is the "discovery that what the child felt as a part of himself is temporarily or permanently lost." In other words, as we have suggested, the first sense of loss is the sense that one has lost *a part of oneself.* The awareness of loss thus gives rise to an *illusion,* because the child imagines that what is no longer attached to the body has "disappeared" and now belongs to "another reality." This is the beginning of the phase of symbiosis, when the child begins to sense that what was experienced as a "coenesthetical part of the self" is not actually a part of the self. The illusion, from Deutsch's perspective, is the child's experience of the loss of the "coenesthetically sensed part of the self" as a loss of a part of one's body.

It is at this point that the "conversion process" begins to evolve. The child wishes to "regain" or to "retrieve" this lost part of himself. He does so by *imagining it.* In other words, as he begins to be deprived of the *illusion* that the mother is a part of himself, as he begins to perceive the existence of objects *separate* from himself, the child immediately generates a *fantasy* that the object is connected to himself. In short, just at the moment that his *illusion* of oneness is beginning to shatter, he compensates by developing a *fantasy* of oneness. The perception of loss is not bearable, it cannot be integrated by the ego. The conversion mechanism means, essentially, that *parts of the body* come to symbolize the lost object. Deutsch states:

> The feeling of object loss [is] a ferment for the symbolization process....each part of the body possesses the potentiality for the symbolic expression of loss and separation. This loss evokes anxiety which, as Freud stated, is a separation anxiety. Hence it calls for replacement. A more highly developed ego turns to different parts of the body which are adequately symbolized and may serve as substitutes for the loss.
> (1959, p. 79)

The body itself, in other words, acts as the *container for the lost other*. Separation of a part of oneself from one's self is denied, and the child fantasizes that the other is still a part of one's self, but now symbolized or *contained in specific bodily parts*. The beloved object, in this way, comes to be "embodied" within the self. This "conversion" of a bodily part, the identification of a part of the body with the mother, leads to the inhibition of function of that body part, or its over-stimulation. The bodily part comes to be "possessed" by the lost object, now introjected into the self. The body has been "taken over" by the object.

It is clear that the conversion process, as described above, resembles closely the mechanism of *internalization*, the fundamental psychic mechanism which describes the process whereby external objects become a part of inner psychic structure. We shall discuss the process of internalization in detail later. Suffice it to say here that if we are correct in comparing the process of internalization to the process of conversion, then the *psychosomatic implications* of internalization must be examined more clearly. Specifically, we are suggesting that the internalized object, even in the normal process of development, must be contained within *specific bodily parts*. The "super-ego" is not only a "psychic structure"; it is a psychosomatic entity; it is "embodied" within.

To summarize: human fantasy begins to evolve as the child perceives that the maternal object is not a part of the self, that the object which provided pleasure and security, and which was experienced as co-extensive with the self, is actually a part of external reality. Consequently, the child begins to *fantasize* about the lost object. This fantasy leads to the mechanism of *conversion*, whereby specific bodily parts come to symbolize or to "contain" the lost other.

The process of conversion is very similar to the mechanism of internalization, whereby the lost object comes to be set up within the self. Insofar as the ego is a body ego, therefore, the internalization of the object leads to the *"possession" of those bodily parts which symbolize the lost object:* the object, contained within the structure of the ego, constitutes a physiological "presence."

Deutsch brings home the essence of the process in the following statement:

> The organic symptom is the protective device against an impending loss of the object which has been retrieved through retrojection and which rests symbolized in the body, where it maintains the body's unity.
>
> (1959, p. 77)

The child is not strong enough to tolerate the experience of the loss of a major part of his ego; such a loss would disrupt the unity of his fragile self. He still requires the illusion of "oneness" with the omnipotently conceived mother. Consequently, in order to avoid the experience of a "mutilated" self, the perception of the separateness of the object leads to "retrojection," whereby the object is "retrieved": it is taken back into the self. This mechanism functions to restore the "unity" of the self. The child is "replenished" by the internalization of the lost object.

Chapter III

The Denial of Separateness

The creation of the human ego as a response to the denial of separateness is a major focus of the work of Norman O. Brown, and is entirely consistent with the theories of symbiosis and conversion which we have presented here. According to Brown:

> The primal act of the human ego is a negative one--not to accept reality, specifically the separation of the child's body from the mother's body.
>
> (1959, p. 160)

Like Deutsch, Brown sees the origin of fantasy in the denial of separation:

> Separation in the present is denied by reactivating fantasies of past union.
>
> (1959, p. 161)

Brown emphasizes, as we have, the *duality* in the structure of the ego, the creation of the human self as a function of the internalization of the other into the self. Brown suggests that

> ...the self is a substitute for the lost other, a substitute which pretends to be the lost other; so that we may embrace ourselves thinking we embrace the mother.
>
> (1959, p. 144)

He quotes Freud, who makes a similar point in *The Ego and the Id:*

> When it happens that a person has to give up a sexual object,

there quite often ensures a modification in his ego which can only be described as a reinstatement of the object within the ego.

(in Brown, 1959, p. 161)

As well as Melanie Klein:

The ego is based on object libido reinvested in the body.

(in Brown, 1959, p. 144)

Brown summarizes this theory of the evolution of psychic structure as follows:

Thus, as a result of object-loss not accepted, the natural self-love of the organism is transformed into the vain project of being both Self and Other, and this project supplies the human ego with its essential energy. When the beloved (parental) object is lost, the love that went out to it is redirected to the self; but since the loss of the beloved object is not accepted, the human ego is able to redirect the human libido to itself only by deluding the libido by representing itself as identical with the lost object.

(1959, p. 161)

The human ego is able to embrace itself, in short, only by deluding itself, only by pretending that *the other exists within the self*.

According to Brown, then, the human ego is created in the flight from separation, in the denial of death. The child is so dependent upon the mother, his attachment to her so intense, that separation from the mother is experienced to be equivalent to the *death of the self*. Rephrased in terms of the theory of symbiosis: the early ego is so identified with the mother, the early experience of the self is so *fused* with the experience and idea of mother, that separation from the mother is experienced as a *loss of self*, as a traumatic shrinkage of one's being. Consequently, in his refusal to abandon connection with the mother, the child internalizes the mother into the self. The denial of separation, therefore, may be thought of as a *refusal to acknowledge the death of that part of the self which was identified with the mother*.

According to Brown, the denial of separateness, and subsequent effort to install the other within the self, is the fundamental act of fantasy:

> It is through fantasy that the ego introjects lost objects and makes identifications. Identifications, as modes of preserving past object-cathexes and thus darkening life in the present with the shadow of the past, are fantasies. Identifications as modes of installing the Other inside the Self are fantasies.
>
> (1959, p. 164)

Brown perceives the dramatic *psychosomatic implications* of the evolution of fantasy:

> Fantasy has the power to alter the body....since life is of the body, fantasy as the negation of life must negate specific bodily organs, so that there can be no fantasy without negation--alteration of the body.
>
> (1959, p. 164)

Deutsch, as we have observed, views the conversion process as an attempt to deny separation by internalizing the object into the body, such that specific bodily parts come to symbolize the lost object. Brown similarly views the process of internalization as a fantasy whereby the object gets into the ego, resulting in the *alteration of the body*. The internalized object becomes identified with parts of the body, and this mechanism functions to "negate specific bodily organs" and to "negate life." The object gets into the ego, the other gets into the self; consequently, the life of the body (and the life of the being who resides within the body) is contaminated.

In other words, we may theorize, insofar as the internalized object becomes a part of one's own body and ego, the individual comes to be "possessed" by the object. The presence (or fantasied presence) of an alien being within comes to thwart the organic unity of the individual, to inhibit one's natural, organismic functioning. So what began as a wish to maintain the unity of self, to avoid the loss of the self by internalizing the other into the self, ends as a negation of the self: the organism is "possessed" by the internalized other, the ego is split into two.

Brown elaborates upon his theory of internalization in *Love's Body* (1966):

> A person is never himself but always a mask; a person never owns his own person, but always represents another by whom he is possessed....one's soul is not one's own.
> (1966, p. 98)

> The soul (self) we call our own is an illusion. The real psychoanalytic contribution to "ego-psychology" is the revelation that the ego is a bit of the outside world swallowed, introjected; or rather a bit of the outside world that we insist on pretending we have swallowed. The nucleus of one's own self is the incorporated other.
> (1966, p. 144)

We are emphasizing, in this monograph, an analysis of the internalization of the mother; but it is obvious that identical psychic mechanisms may be used to describe the process whereby the father is internalized. According to Brown:

> The super-ego is your father in you; your father introjected; your father swallowed. In his most sophisticated description

of super-ego formation, Freud says: "A portion of the external world has, at least partially, been given up as an object and instead, by means of identification, taken into the ego--that is, has become an integral part of the internal world."

(1966, p. 144)

Brown's theory of internalization, then, does not differ substantially from the process of super-ego development as it is conceived in psychoanalytical theory. The difference is this: Brown is suggesting that even in the "normal" case, the impact of the internalization process may not be a benign one. He is not speaking of "unmetabolized internal objects" which may result in clinically defined psychopathology. Rather, Brown is suggesting that the very fact that human beings deny separation and incorporate the other into the self means that *we are all somewhat sick*. This split in the ego, the *loss of self* which is the consequence of the incorporation of the other into the self, is what Brown calls the "universal neurosis of mankind."

To summarize: An internalized object is a mental "sedimentation" of a relationship to another person, an object which gets into the structure of the ego. The motivation for the incorporation of the other into the self is the fear of separation, the fear of the "split" from the mother who is experienced as the omnipotent gratifier of one's needs. By internalizing the object into the self one perpetuates the idea that one is safe and secure, that there is no risk of non-gratification, that one is not alone. The presence of the object within (the fantasy of a "companion" within the self) compensates for the trauma of the loss of the symbiotic state. The internalized object functions to insulate the individual against the vicissitudes of reality.

The internalized object is essentially a cognitive structure, a fantasy. Due, however, to the enormous power of the mother in relation to the child at the time she is internalized, as well as to the physical and physiological closeness of the mother to the child, the object comes to possess a deep, profound "presence" within the self; it is experienced in a psychosomatic way. The self comes to be "possessed" by the internalized other. What began as a mechanism for avoiding the loss of the unity of the self, as a mechanism for maintaining the sense of narcissistic omnipotence, becomes a source of *oppression,* as the organismic unity of body and ego are altered by this alien presence. Organismic functioning is "repressed" or inhibited by the presence of an alien object within the self.

Thus, the fantasy of being a "dual unity," and the subsequent wish to preserve the other within the self results in a significant *mutilation* of the self. The other remains a "foreign body," a "not self," which never can fully be integrated. What began as an effort to maintain the cohesion of the self results in the disruption of the self's cohesion: the internalized object becomes a "weight of oppression," possessing the ego, and altering the natural functioning of the body.

Chapter IV

Internalization

In the following sections I shall examine the psychoanalytic conception of the process of *internalization*, drawing heavily upon the writings of John Frosch, a psychoanalytic clinician. Frosch states:

> Internalization...refers to the process of setting up internal psychic structures, derived from an interplay with external objects. More precisely, it is a shift from the object representation to inclusion in the self-representation.
>
> Via this process, introjections (introjects) are created, and they may be almost anything deriving from the object representation, which in a sense has been abandoned or been lost but whose retention is essential for the organism.
>
> (1983, p. 240)

The criterion for the "normal" outcome of the internalization process, according to Frosch, revolves around the question of the *integration* of the internalized object:

> In the course of normal development and maturation, perhaps with the formation of other introjects, they become integrated into a homogeneous aspect of the psyche, losing (so to speak) their independent and autonomous operation so that ultimately they are not identifiable in their original form. It is then that one may speak of identification, which, by virtue of its integrated state, can under ordinary circumstances no longer be ejected.
>
> (1983, p. 240)

In normal development, then, the introject becomes "integrated into a homogeneous aspect of the psyche," losing its "autonomous operation." Under these circumstances the internalized object becomes *identified* with the overall psychic structure, and thus can no longer be "ejected."

On the other hand, an internalized object may not be integrated. Frosch calls a non-integrated internal object a "true introject":

> The true introject is still to some extent isolated from the rest of the ego and somewhat alien. There is still some separation of the introject from the core self.
>
> (1983, p. 240)

The criterion for a *true introject*, as compared with an integrated internal object, is that it remains *isolated from* the rest of the ego and somewhat alien, it remains separate from the "core self." Such introjects may, according to Frosch, be "ejected" or "projected" during early phases of development. Or they may persist, though unintegrated, into later life, representing a potential for "extrajection" (p. 240).

Frosch draws an analogy between the process of integrating an internal object and the digestion of the food bolus. In the case of the "true introject" the internalized object:

> ...has not yet been digested or metabolized and can be regurgitated....psychic introjects...may remain in the psyche but are perceived as introjects or they may be ejected in the form of persecuting delusions, influencing machines, etc., not too unlike their original source.
>
> (1983, p. 240)

These kinds of introjects correspond to what Kernberg calls "non-metabolized...pathological internalized object relations" (Frosch, p. 240). In the case of identification, on the other hand:

> ...stability of the ego requires that that which is incorporated and introjected eventually become an integral part of the ego, and be integrated into it in a harmonious fashion.
> (1983, p. 240)

Identification implies that:

> ...once the bolus is digested, it enters the blood stream and is metabolized. Ultimately it becomes part of the body chemistry and structure.
> (1983, p. 240)

I do not wish, here, to address the clinical question of the extent to which, and under what circumstances, the internalized object becomes "integrated" into the psyche, and under what circumstances it does not become integrated. I wish, rather, to suggest that this process of internalization may, *even in the course of "normal" development*, have consequences which are negative for the optimal development of human psychic structure.

We have suggested that the object is internalized at a very early phase in development such that it becomes a "psychosomatic presence" within the structure of the ego. We have suggested that, in the conversion process, the internalized object becomes identified with parts of the body, thus functioning to inhibit or overstimulate those body parts. We have hypothesized, in short, that the very presence of an internalized object within the structure of the ego, however inevitable or normal such a development, may function to *negate the self*.

I am, therefore, posing the following question: To what extent can internalized objects genuinely be integrated within the psyche? To what extent does the presence of an "other" within the structure of the ego act or inhibit or arrest development, however "normal" is the process of internalization? In short, I am suggesting that the early symbiotic situation, with the subsequent development of a predisposition toward fantasy and toward the internalization of the object into the ego, may create *a human predisposition toward mental aberration*. It is certainly clear that the concept of "normality" in the human species must be examined within the broader contexts of culture and history. The five thousand-year-old history of human civilizations has witnessed the occurrence of endless wars with millions killed, of civilizations practicing human sacrifice, of genocide based upon the destruction of various "classes" of persons. My own view is that at the root of this human pathology lies the internalization of the object into the self, a mechanism which functions to "cripple" the development of the individuated self.

That is to say: However "normal" is the process of internalization, or introjection, the very presence of an *alien object within the structure of the ego* tends, in my view, to thwart or distort optimal psychic functioning. In other words, if the tendency toward separation-individuation is an *organismic one*, if the movement toward autonomy has a biological root, then the tendency to move toward separation from internalized objects likewise has biological roots.

I would locate the source of this tendency toward organismic integrity in biology, namely in the tendency of the organism to distinguish between self and not-self and to *reject from within the boundaries of the self that which is perceived as not-self*. In other words, just as the organism identifies a bacteria or virus as not-self (a biological act which does not require the conscious mind), so, I would hypothesize, does the human organism identify the internalized object as not-self, with subsequent efforts toward the "rejection" of the internalized object from within the boundaries of the ego. (I would argue, further, that the tendency toward organic integrity on the biological level, and toward autonomy on the psychic level, is paralleled, on the cultural level, in the human *wish to be free*. The human wish for freedom is the wish to possess a self which can *unfold toward the fulfillment of its own developmental destiny,* a tendency which *opposes* forces which would inhibit this natural movement toward the unfolding of the self.)

We know that, in all human cultures, there is a human tendency to internalize the ideas and personalities of other human beings into the self, and that this process is a requirement for the development of the human ego. We know that human cultures embody certain norms, social codes, expected patterns of behavior, etc. This has been described, by anthropologists, sociologists, as well as by psychologists, as the normal process of development within human society. The question which is posed by psychoanalysis, however, is the question of the *psychic price* of socialization. This is the issue which was raised by Freud's book, *Civilization and Its Discontents;* this is the issue raised by Norman O. Brown, when he proposes the idea of the "universal neurosis of mankind." And certainly the *story of human behavior,* as it has been recorded through the years in the history books, warrants that we examine this issue of the "normal" behavior of "cultural man" more thoroughly. What we are suggesting, in this monograph, is that the process of human psychic development is *much more intimately linked with the processes of human cultural development than has ever been acknowledged by psychoanalysis;* that one cannot separate the study of inner psychic development from the study of man *as a cultural being.* The concept of "external reality" is the weakest link in the psychoanalytic explanation of human behavior. The guiding proposition of this study is that "external reality" does not exist as some mystical domain "outside" of human psychic development; that it is not a question of "man," on the one hand, and "reality," on the other. Rather, in my view, *human beings are deeply implicated in the social reality which they create.*

Insofar as I view the process of internalization as a more uncertain and dynamic process than does Frosch I would also, therefore, tend to question Frosch's view that the process of "extrajecting" internal objects is unusual, or abnormal. On the contrary, we shall argue that the process of projecting or extrajecting internal objects is a normal and fundamental mechanism in human development and growth. The tendency toward extrajection, I believe, is linked with the human tendency toward the creation of, and the attachment to, *transitional objects,* objects which serve as *substitutes* for the internalized objects. As the human being struggles to separate, to gain autonomy, to achieve freedom, he struggles to rid himself of the internalized object, which acts as a burden, a weight of oppression. He does so by *projecting* the internalized object onto objects in the external world, thus creating a certain "distance" between one's own ego and the object. To "extraject" the object, therefore, is to distance the object from the self; it is a mechanism toward the development of autonomy.

Chapter V

The Struggle for Separateness

I am suggesting, then, that there is a deep, perhaps biological force within each individual which moves him toward autonomy, toward independence, a force which works toward the evolution of a "true self" which excludes that which is not the self. This force may be equated with the tendency toward "separation-individuation," the tendency of the individual to wish to *separate* from the mother (and from all other objects toward which dependency, or a tendency toward fusion, might develop) and to develop an *individuated* psychic structure, a psychic structure which is individual or distinct, *differentiated from others of the same species*. To individuate means to develop as an *individual*, as a distinct and separate organic unit.

On the other hand, as we have noted, the attachment to the *fantasy of oneness*, the attachment to the fantasy of the omnipotent mother, the refusal to separate from the mother, is an equally powerful force in human development. The human ego does *not wish to differentiate itself*, does not wish to experience itself as a *separate* or separated unit. The pleasures associated with the intimacy with the mother are deeply fixed within the psyche. At the same time that there is a wish for separateness and autonomy, there is simultaneously a *refusal* to separate, a refusal to abandon the attachment to the mother, a refusal to become autonomous, since autonomy means separation from one's primary source of pleasure, security and identity. The tendency toward separation-individuation, therefore, I would hypothesize, always occurs in relation to the tendency toward symbiosis. Consequently, the human being exists, throughout his life, in a state of *conflict:* a conflict between the wish to separate, the wish to move forward, the wish to become more autonomous, on the one hand; and the wish for symbiosis, the wish to move backward, the regressive longing to "return" to the maternal matrix, on the other.

It is for this reason that I use the word *struggle* to describe the human effort to achieve separation and separateness: the struggle is against *one's own wish not to separate*. In other words, however powerful or natural is the striving for separation and individuation, the attraction toward the infantile fantasy of merger is equally strong. Consequently, the process (or project) of separating is forever intermingled with regressive longings, and burdened with questions such as the following: Is it worth the struggle? Is it worth it to become a separate individual, an individuated self, if this means I must abandon the "infantile paradise," abandon the pleasures and security associated with the attachment to mother (and toward other dependently cathected objects)? The process of separation-individuation, in short, is *fraught with ambivalence*.

Further, I would hypothesize, due to the power of the merger fantasy and of regressive longings, the *achievement of a reasonable degree of autonomy is problematic for human beings*. My own observations lead me to believe that a reasonable degree of autonomy is *not achieved by most human beings along many dimensions;* that the fear of separateness is so powerful in human beings, the need for dependent attachment so intense, the need to "connect" to an omnipotent object so inescapable, that most human beings exist in a state of *developmental arrest*. Their *attachments to objects* (and, as we shall see, toward symbols of these objects), their wish for fusion, means that the *process of separation-individuation becomes blocked*, the ego becomes stunted, growth is arrested.

Still, to turn the coin over once again, in spite of the dependent attachments, the human being struggles toward autonomy. M. D. Faber describes this struggle, vividly, as follows:

> From one perspective the whole task of infancy and childhood is getting separate, getting independent, getting autonomous. As is generally known, the majority of human beings struggle and stumble toward that condition throughout the course of their lives. Indeed, the inclination to alter one's ordinary awareness, to achieve another kind of consciousness, is largely an *inclination to go beyond the early time and beyond the indviduals who make up that time.* At the deepest level, it is *the inclination to have oneself.*
>
> (1981, pp. 62-3)

Faber, in this passage, connects the process of separation-individuation to the issue of the *self*. I would elaborate upon this as follows: however attractive the fantasy of merger, however tempting the pleasures of regressive attachment and dependency, there is a deep sense in which such psychic tendencies are experienced as a *mutilation of the self*, as a loss of freedom, a sense of bondage. To "have oneself" is to have a self which is autonomous, free from dependent attachment to objects, and this means separateness and freedom from *internalized* objects as well.

That is to say: The ego, we have observed, is originally a body ego. Yet, as a consequence of the early, symbiotic illusion, the child imagines that *his mother's body is part of his own body,* a "dual unity" of child and mother, two separate organisms existing within a common boundary. This tendency to incorporate a *second unit* into the self (the duality of the human ego) is perpetuated when the *internalized object* is incorporated into the ego.

The mother remains, however, in spite of the fantasy of the child, a *separate individual*. However "close" she may be to the child, however deep the intimacy he experiences in relation to her, she remains a *completely discrete biological entity*; once birth occurs, the organic connection between child and mother is severed forever. Thus, I would suggest, insofar as the mother "gets inside" the child, or is *experienced* as being inside the child, she is experienced as a "not self," as an object which "does not belong inside." Consequently, there is an organismic tendency toward the *rejection of the mother*, the function of which is to "have one's self," to have a self which contains nothing which is alien to the self. This tendency toward freedom and autonomy, toward a unified body and self, works toward the *removal or rejection from the self of that which is not genuinely the self*. The existence of such a tendency means that, in spite of the depth and intensity of primitive internalizations, there is a tendency toward *undoing* these internalizations.

Chapter VI

The Fantasy of Merger as a Source of Anxiety

The fantasy of merger, we have observed, is associated with the dream of omnipotence and effortless gratification, as well as with the denial of external reality. This fantasy, we may suggest, is the source of the *dream of paradise* which is such a common theme in mythology, art and literature, as well as of many political ideologies. Once separated from the state of symbiotic oneness, the child does not abandon the dream of narcissistic omnipotence. Rather, he continues to fantasize the "return" of the narcissistic state. The dream of paradise, from this point of view, is the *regressive wish to reunite with the mother, projected forward* into the idea of some "future state," or condition, where the infantile situation will be recovered, or recaptured. The struggles waged by many human beings, struggles to attain some "dream" in the future, often reflect this tendency to "move backward by moving forward": it is a fantasy of unlimited gratification or bliss in the future, modelled upon the infantile state of oneness or symbiosis, which serves as a crucial *motivation for development*. One expects that, upon the achievement of some aspiration or the attainment of some goal, one will be "rewarded" by the return of the narcissistic condition.

For many individuals, of course, this "dream of re-fusion" remains an unconscious dream, co-existing with reality-oriented behavior. For more disturbed individuals on the other hand, the merger fantasy may come to dominate psychic life. In such cases, it would appear, the "realization" of the fantasy of re-fusion or merger is experienced, not as a "return to paradise," but as the source of intense anxiety. Activation of the merger fantasy is associated with the *loss of the self*. Frosch states:*

> Blurring of ego boundaries and dedifferentiation may be a step toward recapturing the breast, making the nourishing object a part of the self. Yet this is not an unmixed gain for the psychotic, as there is also the danger of being engulfed by the object.
> (1983, p. 212)

This view, that cathexis of the fantasy of dedifferentiation and the loss of a sense of ego-boundaries is a fundamental source of human anxiety, would appear to be shared by a number of psychoanalytic theorists. Thus, Loewald speaks of "primary identity," i.e., the fantasy of union with the mother, as the source of the "deepest dread":

> The original unity and identity, undifferentiated and unstructured, of the psychic apparatus and environment, is as much of a danger for the ego as the demand of the "paternal castration threat" to give it up altogether.
> (1983, quoted in Frosch, p. 212)

Schur states, similarly:

> The simultaneous tendency for refusion of the self and object representation and for vagueness of self boundaries constitutes

---

* In the following discussion, when I speak of the fantasy of merger, I am focusing upon the fantasy of merger as it relates to *internal objects*, as well as to objects in the external world. The sense of the *fusion of the self with the internalized object* is suggested in the following passage: "When the object is omnipotently incorporated, the self becomes so identified with the incorporated object that all separate identity or any boundary between self and object is denied" (Rosenfeld, quoted in Frosch, 1983, p. 247).

the greatest threat to the maintenance of reality, to females as well as males.
(quoted in Frosch, 1983, p. 211)

The anxiety associated with the fantasy of merger would appear to be connected with the sense of the *loss of self*. Thus, Modell states:

> When there is intense fear of merging with a "bad" object the subject may fear a loss of identity, dread of being influenced, and ultimately may fear complete annihilation.
> (quoted in Frosch, 1983, p. 211)

And Kaplan, discussing the child's fantasy of oneness, states:

> Were he to succumb to the absolute bliss of oneness before carving out his own space in the world, the child would be reabsorbed into the being of his mother. His surrender would be tantamount to ceasing to exist.
> (1978, pp. 172-173)

The following statement made by a patient in psychoanalytic treatment gives some of the clinical feeling of this dread of merger:

> Do you know the difference between closeness, likeness, sameness and oneness? Close is close, as with you; when you are like the other, but he is still he and you are you; but oneness is not two, it is one, that's horrible, horrible--don't get too close, get away from the couch, I don't want to be you.
> (Jacobson, quoted in Frosch, 1983, p. 214)

This report is interesting, since it indicates that the fantasy of oneness, the dream of regressive fusion or de-differentiation, the dream of symbiosis, is pleasurable as long as the boundaries of the ego are strong enough such that the fusion fantasy remains a *fantasy*. When there is ego-weakness, when there is fragility in the structure of the ego, the idea of a "return" to the non-differentiated state *does not seem to be anticipated with the slightest degree of pleasure.* When there is the danger of a "breakdown" in the experience of ego boundaries, what is elicited is anxiety and dread.

Frosch relates the danger of dedifferentiation, in psychotic and borderline psychotic patients, to the "total loss of self":

> It is the possibility that dedifferentiation might eventuate in total loss of self that makes it so frightening to the psychotic or borderline psychotic. This threat may be especially frightening because the possibility of reversal is minimal. In the normal person and in the neurotic, the blurring of ego boundaries and dedifferentiation may be tolerated in the belief that ultimately ego boundaries can be reestablished intact. It resembles regression in the service of the ego (or under ego control), as there is always the awareness of enough capacity for ego integration to reverse dedifferentiation. In the psychotic, however, since the chance of reversal is less, the process of dedifferentiation may really eventuate in dissolution of the self.
>
> (1983, p. 215)

Thus, according to Frosch, while the blurring of ego-boundaries in the normal individual is seen to be a temporary situation, comparable to "regression under the control of the ego," in psychotics the process of dedifferentiation, or the loss of ego-boundaries, is perceived to represent a threat which will be non-reversible and which will result in the "dissolution of the self." In attempting to understand why some of his patients experience such overwhelming fear, Frosch describes one of them who seemed to express it best. He sums up his impression of the nature of her anxiety:

> It was not quite death of just dying; it was disappearing, nothingness, being completely engulfed and dissolving.
>
> (1983, p. 215)

It is clear, then, that in spite of the prevalence of *fantasies of merger* and of a return to the state of symbiosis, when the *actualization* of this fantasy is perceived to be a possibility, the experience is not anticipated with pleasure. On the contrary, intense anxiety is elicited. Further, as we have observed, a number of psychoanalytic theorists view this idea of a return to the "undifferentiated" condition as constituting one of the primary sources of anxiety for the human being, insofar as the idea of a state of oneness is associated with the "loss of self."

Thus, alongside the dream of "dual unity," the dream of the recovery of narcissistic omnipotence, etc., which we have discussed earlier, we must now place the *fear of regression,* the intense anxiety associated with the loss of the boundaries of the ego, which may be equated with being "dragged down" into the realm of the mother and losing one's separate identity. Opposing the wish to "connect" with an omnipotent object, to attach to objects in the world which promise power and pleasure, must be placed the human desire to *maintain the intactness of ego-boundaries,* to maintain the *separation of the self* from objects in the external world (as well as from internal objects) which would threaten to deprive the ego of its intactness, cohesiveness, and integrity.

The "struggle" which we have described previously, then, the conflict between the attachment to the fusion fantasy and the wish for separation-individuation, may be viewed also as a conflict between the *wish* for fusion and the *fear* of fusion. The intensity of the struggle to separate, from this point of view, reflects not only the positive thrust toward individuation and growth, but reflects, as well, the fear of a psychic posture which is experienced as a *threat to one's survival*. The individual struggles, fights to separate, because regression to the maternal matrix is associated with the *death of the self*. The nature of this conflict becomes even more complex, and its resolution more difficult, when we recall that the beloved maternal object is *internalized* at a very early age. Thus we may ask: How is it possible to maintain the boundaries of one's ego when the threat to the loss of boundaries emanates from an object which is *inside the self*? How can one achieve separateness from an object which is imagined to be *contained within the structure of one's own ego*?

Chapter VII

Conflict and Ambivalence
Surrounding Separation-Individuation

We have suggested, then, that the process of separation-individuation, while perhaps being a reflection of a fundamental, organismic tendency, is by no means a natural or inevitable process. Rather, we have put forth the view that the movement toward separation-individuation is a process *fraught with conflict and ambivalence;* that it generates an intense *struggle* within the individual; and that the achievement of a favorable outcome, a reasonable degree of autonomy, is quite problematic.

We have hypothesized that a basic source of the human ambivalence toward separation-individuation is the *attachment to the fantasy of symbiosis,* the persisting attraction of the maternal matrix, which causes the human being to experience separation and growth as the loss of something precious; to individuate is simultaneously to *abandon paradise.* One wonders if separation and growth is worth the effort, since individuation means that one will have to abandon the "connection" to the mother, which has seemed to mean the immediate and effortless gratification of one's desires.

We have also noted that, just as there is an intense conflict between the progressive, individuating tendencies and the regressive, symbiotic tendencies, so is there intense ambivalence surrounding the fusion fantasy itself. On the one hand, it seems to promise "paradise." On the other hand, in order to experience this state of "oneness," one must abandon the boundaries of one's differentiating ego; to do so is intensely feared, since such an ego state is associated with the dissolution of the self. The ambivalence surrounding the regressive fantasy of merger may be observed in Frosch's analysis of one of his patients:

> On the one hand, the patient wished to be closer to, to merge with her mother. Yet this was accompanied by a tremendous dread, bringing in its wake the fear of overwhelming natural forces which she could not control. She feared that she would disintegrate and disappear, just as the universe would. The hostility and ambivalence toward the mother contained the possibility of destruction of the mother. It brought in its wake the possibility of her own disintegration because of the self-not-self confusion. Automatically her very world would disintegrate.
> (1983, pp. 314-315)

On the one hand, the patient experiences "tremendous dread," a "fear of overwhelming natural forces which she could not control," a fear that she, as well as the universe, would "disintegrate and disappear." Yet, in spite of these reactions to the wish for merger with the mother, *this does not cause her to abandon this wish*. Rather, she still wishes "to be closer to, to merge with the mother." One can observe, in this description, the power of the ambivalent wish, the fact that the symbiotic situation continues to be desired in spite of the fact that it is the source of such intense psychic pain.

The tendency of the human being to *idealize* the idea of fusion may be observed in the following statement made by the same patient:

> Even if I died, I would still be with her. I would be in her thoughts. We would never be separated.
> (1983, p. 315)

This idea of two human beings "never being separated," the idea of two human beings existing in each others' thoughts, a spiritual connection which persists and which defies physical separation, would appear to be a significant element of the idea of "romance," which is a central feature of Western civilization. What is expressed in the "dream of romantic love" is a kind of intense, spiritual bond between two persons, which connects them in a state of "oneness." The fantasy of *bodily union* associated with the symbiotic fantasy is replaced by a sense of *spiritual union,* a oneness of thoughts, which assures that two persons will be eternally "together."

The idea of fusion through love is a major theme of Western music, particularly of American popular music. Phrases such as "Two hearts beating as one," "I can't live without your love," and "If you leave me, I'll die," recurring endlessly in the history of popular music, seem to express the fusion fantasy, the idea that two persons can experience one another as if "one"; and to express the idea that to *separate* from the experience of oneness is tantamount to the death of the self. Romantic love, as it has been depicted in the history of Western culture, would seem to revolve around the *spiritualization* of the symbiotic fantasy, the idea that two separate beings can experience their lives as if in unity, as if connected by a magical, spiritual bond; and that, to separate from one's love object is to separate from the source of one's existence.

Romantic love, however, I would argue, is only one of many cultural ideologies in which the dream of fusion is embodied and expressed. I do not wish to examine these here. Suffice it to say that there is an abundance of material appearing in human literature, music, art, etc., which suggests that the human being is *profoundly unwilling to abandon the dream of narcissistic omnipotence,* profoundly unwilling to abandon the fantasy of fusion, the fantasy of being "together" with another human being. And that this *refusal* persists, in spite of the human perception of the *self-destructive* aspects of this wish. Human beings know, on some level, that to *embrace* the fusion fantasy is to renounce one's autonomy, to be threatened with the mutilation of the self. Yet, in spite of the negative consequences which are anticipated, this *does not prevent human beings from continuing to embrace and to idealize the symbiotic dream.* On the simplest level, persons continue to "love their mothers," and to idealize maternal love. The symbiotic dream would appear to possess a "sacred" quality for many human beings, and persons will often *cling to this attachment,* perpetuate it at all costs, in spite of the destructive consequences.

So the *refusal* to separate from the mother, the refusal to abandon the dream of "oneness," combined with the desire to separate and to individuate, puts the human being in a deep *bind.* This ambivalent posture constitutes, I believe, the fundamental matrix for human development; but it is simultaneously a potentially *explosive* situation. The problem, and the source of the ambivalence, is that the idealized fantasy of "perfect love," of eternal union with the mother, is simultaneously the source of the *loss of one's power,* the loss of one's capacity to grow and develop. The idealized dream of oneness is, in actuality, a manifestation of a *dependent, infantile attachment.* This dependent attachment stands in the way of growth and development, oppresses the self as it reaches toward its own powers.

This is not the place to examine in detail the ambivalent attachment to the mother, and its consequences. But I wish to explore it briefly here. In *The Psychoanalysis of Racism, Revolution and Nationalism* (Koenigsberg, 1977), we interpreted the revolutionary behavior patterns of Hitler, Lenin and Sri Aurobindo as constituting a *struggle against passivity*. I would now view their patterns of revolutionary behavior as a *counterphobic defense against the regressive fantasy of merger*. Hitler is deeply attached to "Germany," Lenin to "the people"--these are the symbolic equivalents of the symbiotic mother. Hitler wishes to be "one" with Germany; Lenin wishes to be one with "the people." Each of them idealizes the object of his love, and believes that any action undertaken is justifiable if done in the name of this love-object. Hitler will undertake any activity in the name of the betterment of the "German nation"; Lenin believes that any activity is justifiable if it will result in the improvement of the condition of "the people."

In each case, however, it would appear that the *other side* of the idealized wish for union with the object is a *passive dependency,* which I would interpret as the psychic consequence of the infantile, symbiotic attachment to the mother. The passive-dependent wish is *projected* onto other objects in social reality, various "classes" of persons, and the effort is then made to "kill" one's dependency by killing the object which symbolizes the dependency. The object which is killed is, in my view, the *infantile, symbiotic ego as it attaches to the omnipotent mother*. Revolutionaries such as Hitler and Lenin are trying to "kill off" that part of themselves which symbolizes their dependent, symbiotic attachment. But they have undertaken an impossible task because the wish to *preserve the symbiotic bond* (in the form of an attachment to symbolic equivalents such as the nation or the people) is *precisely what fuels the revolutionary struggle*. The revolution is a revolution, an active thrust into reality, *against* the regressive attachment. It is the attachment which *fuels the revolution,* both as it is reflected in the wish to perpetuate the state of oneness (e.g., Hitler and Lenin insist that *nothing exists in separation from the state,* the idea of the nation embodies the dream of oneness, or totality), and in the struggle against the consequences of embracing the symbiotic dream (e.g., Hitler and Lenin refuse to be "pinned down," to be "oppressed," etc.). The "revolutionary," in short, according to this view, is one who simultaneously *refuses to relinquish the symbiosis and who struggles against the burden of the symbiosis.* Thus "stuck in the middle," his revolutionary struggle is "permanent."

In short, the *ambivalence toward the symbiotic mother,* due to the wish for fusion which she elicits, is a fundamental aspect of the process of separation-individuation. On the one hand the mother is "loved," as the idealized, omnipotent protector of the child, as the "guarantee" of gratification. On the other hand, as the child develops, she is "hated," *precisely because she elicits the symbiotic fantasy,* which now must be "rejected" as the child moves toward independence.

The anger or hostility may be viewed as a *reaction-formation against the passive attachment,* a way of warding off the symbiotic attachment, pushing the mother away, an attempt to "kill off" the mother, which is really an attempt to destroy the dependent attachment to her. It also represents an effort to destroy or to "lop off" a part of one's self, the ego which is symbiotically tied to the omnipotent mother. The hostility (and this can be perceived clearly in the case of revolutionaries such as Hitler and Lenin) is an attempt to "cut" the symbiotic bond, to "smash" the dependency, to "liberate oneself" from the oppressive object to which one is attached. What "oppresses" is *precisely the burden of one's own dependent attachment.* The attachment to an omnipotent object may make the ego feel "bigger" (e.g., a primary identification with "Germany" as a substitute for the primary identification with the mother); but the internalization of such a massive object into the self also *weighs one down;* it is a *heavy burden* to carry such an object within. So the wish to destroy the object, the hostility and the anger experienced in relationship to the object, represents a wish to *liberate oneself* from the object which is the source of one's oppressive, dependent attachment. When Hitler acts, in the end, toward the destruction of Germany, one of his motives, I believe, is to *free himself from the burden of his attachment to Germany,* to destroy the object which has held him "in thrall" for so many years, to "sever" the symbiotic bond which has connected him to this symbolic mother. If Hitler destroys himself at the same time that he destroys Germany, it is because he has so irrevokably committed himself to the dream of symbiotic oneness. Hitler and Germany remain "fused" as the world war ends, embracing one another in the fire of war and death.

To summarize our argument as it now stands: The symbiotic situation, with all of its pleasures and gratifications, gives way to the developmental wish to individuate, to become a separate, autonomous self. As the child begins to perceive his "separateness" from the mother, however, he is traumatized: his ego, at that moment, is too weak to accept the blow of separation; he cannot deal with the loss of omnipotence, and with the perception of his "shrunken" state of being. Consequently, the *fantasy of merger* develops, the fantasy that one is still connected to, still exists in a state of "oneness" with, the mother. This fantasy is perpetuated when the child *internalizes* the object into his own psychic structure.

The movement toward separation-individuation, because of the human unwillingness to abandon the infantile "paradise," is fraught with conflict and ambivalence. The conflict, in the first place, is between the wish for progression versus the wish for regression, the wish for autonomy and a differentiated ego versus the wish for "oneness." But the conflict also stems from ambivalence surrounding the regressive dream: while it seems to promise power, instant gratification, bodily pleasure, it also implies the *loss of self*. To return to a state of "oneness" is to lose the boundaries of one's personality. Thus, however powerful are the regressive longings, these fantasies elicit a *reaction against them,* which may be described as a *struggle* for independence, a struggle to *overcome* the dream of symbiosis and to achieve autonomy. The *struggle* for separation-individuation, in short, reflects the fact that this tendency develops in the matrix of an *opposing* tendency.

So the human being begins his life's journey. As he strives to fulfill his "developmental destiny" he is departing from a state of "oneness," and moving to become a separated, autonomous being. But his deep attraction to the symbiotic fantasy means that the achievement of his developmental destiny will not come easily, that his effort to do so will involve an intense struggle. What is difficult, in particular, is the *length of time* which must pass before he is actually in a position to be autonomous. In spite of being a "separate" individual, the child's ego is so fragile, and his *actual* dependency so real, that it will be a long time before he can exercise his autonomy with any genuine effectiveness. So the question is, how can he "bridge the gap" between his early phase of dependence, and the achievement of autonomy, which will come much later? How will the human being handle the time "in between?"

The child begins to separate from the illusion of symbiosis. But he is not yet strong enough to give up this "magical" state; he is unable, and unwilling, to renounce the dream of omnipotence. So the issue is: How can he *get away* from the symbiotic mother without being forced to renounce the omnipotent fantasies which are associated with the mother? How can one give up the illusion of total security (which had been able to flower for so long, due to the nearly absolute dependence of the child upon the mother) without plunging headlong into a confrontation with the reality of insecurity? How can one *abandon* the attachment to the mother without having to abandon the attachment? Or: How can one move toward separation-individuation without having to abandon the symbiotic fantasy, which provides a kind of "base of security"? We have noted one of the *fundamental* resolutions to this problem, which is the mechanism of *internalization*. By *internalizing* the omnipotent object the individual moves toward separation from one's actual mother, and from one's family, but continues to preserve the object within as part of one's psychic structure. The internalized object is a "companion," which "accompanies" the individual as he moves toward autonomy. It is a source of sustenance, solace, and narcissistic supplies; the internalized "body" of the mother constitutes a source of nourishment as one begins the arduous trip toward autonomy.

But I would like to propose the existence of another mechanism which is equally fundamental in human psychic development, a mechanism which we shall explore through the rest of this monograph. What I am now hypothesizing, and shall attempt to demonstrate, is that the struggle to escape the "gravitational pull" of the maternal matrix is enhanced by the existence of various institutionalized, cultural forms, whose basic function is to act as a "centripetal force," to draw the individual away from the infantile "paradise," to encourage him to abandon the symbiotic attachment to the mother and to move forward into reality. These mechanisms are *built into the social structure,* they are forms which already exist within the society; to reveal the nature and meaning of these forms is to *reveal their psychic function, t*o show the manner in which they function as a "link" between the infantile ego and the maturing ego. The function of such social forms, I shall argue, is to *assist the individual in breaking the spell of the symbiotic fantasy,* and thus to permit the individual to move forward into reality. "Society," from this point of view, functions as a *defense against regression.* But it cannot merely "squelch" this fantasy; the fantasy is far too powerful. Rather, it must use the dream of symbiosis, sequester the libidinal and psychic energy attached to it, by creating possibilities for the *displacement* of this fantasy.

Social forms, in other words, we shall argue, function to provide a "solution" to the "impossible" conflict described above: the conflict between the wish to progress and the wish to regress; between the wish for omnipotence and the wish to become a human individual; between the wish to "connect" and the wish to separate; between the wish for omnipotent fusion and the wish to abandon this desire. Social forms, we hypothesize, represent humanly created, institutionalized "solutions," whose purpose is to answer questions such as the following: How can one give up the dream of omnipotence and at the same time perpetuate it? How can one become a separate individual without giving up one's dream of connectedness? How can one perpetuate the experience of oneness, the dream of fusion, without losing one's self? Human cultural forms, in short, are designed to "get one out" of the narcissistic bind, to pull one away from the symbiotic bond; but, at the same time, to soften the blow, to provide "consolation"; indeed, in many instances, to pretend that separation has never actually occurred.

Chapter VIII

The Transitional Object and the Struggle to Separate

The concept of the "transitional object" has become increasingly important in current psychoanalytic thought. This is not the place to review the growing body of literature on this subject. Rather, let us simply present one of the early, classic statements of this concept, and see if we may connect it to the ideas presented in this monograph and hence to a general theory of the psychological roots of culture. Arnold Modell describes the transitional object as follows:

> The transitional human object is an object that stands midway between what is created by the inner world and that which exists in the environment. The transitional object is not completely created by the individual, it is not a hallucination; it is an object "in" the environment. It is something other than the self, but the separateness from the self is only partially acknowledged, since the object is given life by the subject. It is a created environment--created in the sense that the properties attributed to the object reflect the inner life of the subject.
> (1968, p. 35)

Put somewhat differently:

> The transitional object is a substitute for the actual environment--a substitute that creates the illusion of encapsulating the subject from the dangers of the environment.
> (1968, p. 35)

We have observed that one of the fundamental dilemmas of human existence is the issue of separation from the omnipotent, symbiotic mother. This issue of human development constitutes a *dilemma* because it is so fraught with conflict and ambivalence: conflict between the wish to progress toward independence versus the wish to remain in a state of dependent attachment; ambivalence surrounding the fantasy of fusion itself, which is intensely idealized on the one hand, but deeply feared on the other. We have suggested that the psychological structure of this conflict or dilemma constitutes a "bind" for the human being and that without a mechanism for resolving the dilemma the human being might get "stuck," he might become paralyzed, unable to develop. We have hypothesized, therefore, that one of the ways in which human beings attempt to resolve this dilemma, attempt to get out of this bind, is through the use of various social forms or cultural mechanisms whose purpose is to *ease the transition* from one psychic place to another psychic place. The *transitional object,* specifically, is that object which permits the individual to *transfer or project* the psychic energy and affects which had been bound up with the omnipotent mother into external reality. The transitional object is the object which inherits the attachment to the mother, and which thus permits the *transfer of libidinal energy.* The transitional object assists the human being in resolving the psychic dilemma because it stands "midway between what is created by the inner world and that which exists in the environment."

The transitional object is that object which permits the individual to *leave* the mother because this object *symbolizes* the mother, or is endowed with some of the "magical" properties of the omnipotent object. In the *absence* of the beloved object, the individual creates a "dream of love," a fantasy which preserves the idea or memory of the beloved object. When these inner emotions are projected into objects which have an existence as a modality of culture, they become *shared transitional objects.*

Let us briefly attempt to clarify the transitional mechanism by looking at the phenomenon of music. A "love song," for example, hummed or imagined by a given individual, may serve as a transitional object. One is dreaming of the beloved object, and this dream is concretized in terms of a melody or song. If the song which one is humming is a *popular* song, then one's own dream of love may be *shared;* there exists, in the culture, a *shared vehicle for expressing the dream of love.* The song is a *shared* transitional object. If this song exists as a *record,* we can see the meaning of Modell's definition above: the object exists "in" the environment, it is an "external object." But it is not an external object in the way psychoanalysts have usually thought of external objects: as objects in reality which exist apart from the subject. Rather, the song, or the record, is a "created environment," in the sense that its properties "reflect the inner life of the subject." Of course, given this perspective, one must immediately pose the following question: do *any* of the objects of culture exist in a purely "external" sense; do not *all* objects of culture "reflect the inner life of the subject?" In short, if we may conceptualize a piece of music as a transitional object, may we not consider the possibility that *all of the objects of culture function as transitional objects?*

But let us focus here upon the function of the transitional object as serving to *get the child away from the symbiotic object,* to provide a *modus operandi* for separating from the object, and for transferring psychic energy *away* from the fusion fantasy and the maternal matrix, and into external reality.

The transitional object may be viewed as a substitute for the symbiotic mother, an externalized representation of the "symbiotic half of the self." The transitional object is like an "externalized internal object." Instead of *internalizing* the object as a response to loss, setting up the object as a psychic structure within one's own mind/body (the psychosomatic conversion symptom), the object is perpetuated in the form of an *external symbol of the object.* The object is now on the "borderline" between internal and external; it is something "other than the self;" but "the separateness from the self" is only partially acknowledged. The object is "given life by the subject"; it is cathected only insofar as it is a substitute for the love-object.

As a substitute for the symbiotic fantasy from which the child has unwillingly separated, therefore, the transitional object functions to provide "solace" (Horton, 1981), to make separation bearable. The transitional object is endowed with some of the magical, comforting properties of the maternal object. (The teddybear is still an excellent example of a transitional object. The child clings to this "external object" as if it were a part of himself. He endows it with various properties of lovableness, lovingness, etc., even though it is an inanimate object. The teddybear provides a sense of comfort and security. And it may serve as the "container" for various fantasies surrounding love and affection, substituting for maternal affection and comfort, which is now perceived to be not always available.) The child "clings" to the transitional object and experiences it as an *extension of his self;* it is a container for his fantasies of *connectedness.* It is an external object, but it is an object which exists within the boundaries of his inner psychic space.

It is our view that the creation of transitional objects is one of the fundamental human mechanisms in terms of which development occurs. We have noted the highly ambivalent and conflictual nature of the separation-individuation process, due to the child's unwillingness to separate from the symbiotic mother, which has constituted such an enormous part of his ego and his identity. The transitional object serves to *make separation bearable* insofar as the *new* object is *endowed with the omnipotent properties* of the first object. The transitional objects which permit the child to "bridge the gap" from an attachment to the mother to an involvement with external reality are "new" in a sense. But they are also "old" insofar as they are *perceived in the image of the early love-object*. The transitional object functions to "contain" the affects, the illusions, the overall perceptual structure which developed in relation to the symbiotic mother. The object thus permits the child to *sever* the attachment to the mother, but only under the condition that he can *perpetuate* this attachment, insofar as the new object is a *symbol* of the omnipotent mother, to which the child is mystically "connected." Thus, by transferring his fantasies and psychic energy from one transitional object to another, the individual can "move along" in his development *without, however, abandoning the psychic bond with or attachment to the symbiotic object*. Separation is achieved, the ego can accept separation, only under the condition that it is *not actually abandoning the fantasy of omnipotence*. Development occurs under the assumption that one is *moving from one omnipotent object to another,* leaving one "realm of omnipotence" in order to enter into another realm of omnipotence. The fantasy of omnipotence is never abandoned. But developmental movement is achieved insofar as the *object* upon which the fantasy of omnipotence is projected changes.

For example, the fantasy of being connected to an omnipotent object may be displaced, in the ordinary process of development, from the mother to the father. The father *inherits t*he fantasy of omnipotence, which first developed in relationship to the symbiotic mother. But he is a more *distant,* and therefore safer, omnipotent object. There is less danger of being "engulfed" by the father, i.e., there is less danger of being engulfed by the mother (which is the situation most deeply feared) if the father can serve, in her stead, as the "container" for the dream of omnipotent connectedness.

Subsequently, in American culture, the adolescent may attach his omnipotent fantasies to a *baseball team,* to which he becomes attached. He links his own identity with the idea of "his team," an object which exists as a part of the external world. The fantasy of omnipotence, through this mechanism, *gets him out* into social reality: he follows his team in the newspapers, reads books about baseball, learns mathematics in order to compute "batting averages,"* plays baseball himself. But the *motivation for his involvement* remains the dream of narcissistic omnipotence, the dream of being "connected" to a powerful object, which functions as a substitute for the infantile object. The "symbolic object," the baseball team, functions as a *transitional object,* functions to permit the individual to *displace* the psychic energy which had been bound up internally onto an object which exists in social reality. The function of the transitional object, here, is to *facilitate the shift in cathectic energy*.

The mechanism of externalization or "extrajection" or projection thus permits the *regressive attachment to act as a progressive force.* This mechanism, I believe, is *built into the very fabric or structure of society.* That is to say, it is not sufficient to conceptualize this process by stating that

---

*The dream of omnipotence motivates *intellectual development*.

the individual "uses" the objects of culture as transitional objects. Rather, what I am suggesting is that the *very meaning of culture,* the very nature of its structure and form, develops by virtue of its capacity to provide this psychic function. The culture (and all cultures differ in the *nature of the pattern* which they provide; each is a *different solution)* exists as an already "tested" pattern of transitional solutions, and thus the individual's own psychic development is *intimately bound up with the structure of his culture.* The culture defines the *nature* of the transitional solutions. To grow up in a particular culture, therefore, is to be strongly inclined to "plug in" to the transitional solutions which the culture provides.

To "plug in" to a culture, then, is to "move along" from one transitional object to another, to transfer one's omnipotent attachments from one symbolic object to another. For an educated person, the cultural objects to which he attaches may be books, works of art, music, ideologies, etc. For an "ordinary" person, on the other hand, the objects of attachment may be sports heroes, movie stars, popular music, etc. In either case, the objects permit the individual to "move along" from one psychic place to another by permitting him to *transfer* his fantasy of omnipotence from one object to another. The omnipotent object to which he is attached, the object with which he identifies, provides a kind of "anchor" for his identity.

We shall focus, in subsequent sections of this monograph, on one particular transitional object which is highly significant in contemporary culture in providing an anchor for identity: the country, or nation. This is a fundamental symbolic object in modern life, serving, for great numbers of persons, as a "container" for the dream of omnipotence, the dream of symbiotic fusion. Adrift in the world, once separated from his family, the individual becomes an "American," a "German," a "Frenchman." He *fuses* his identity with this new omnipotent object. He identifies with it, as he once identified with the omnipotent mother. He "re-connects" with the omnipotent mother by connecting with his country. By linking one's own sense of self with this massive transitional object, the individual is striving to "recapture" infantile omnipotence.

What is interesting about the human tendency to attach to transitional objects and is an important aspect of the mechanism, I believe, is the tendency to perceive the object as existing "out there," as having an objective existence in the world, as being part of "external reality." Even though we cannot point to a particular referent in reality which equates with it, we tend to experience the country, for example, as existing "out there," somewhere external to us. We rarely tend to experience the nation as existing "in here," within ourselves, as a psychic structure that exists because we have created it, as an idea which reflects the "inner life of the subject."

This is, in a sense, the change in perspective which I am suggesting in this monograph: that we begin to "re-connect" human cultural objects with the beings who have created them, and who continue to use them. That we begin to recognize that *it all begins with the self,* it all begins in human psychic structure, the entire "world" which exists "out there" is not some "external" domain, foreign to man; rather it is a world which man has created, a world which is a response to his own needs and fears. It is a world which is consistent with his psychic structure, it *reflects* his psychic structure; it was created by man to *assist him in the development of his psychic structure.* To say that "culture determines," therefore, is only a small part of the story.

What is occurring is that culture is *providing:* it is providing objects, institutions, ideologies, processes which represent time-tested "solutions," methods which man has discovered or invented for resolving his transitional dilemmas.

Culture is a human creation or invention. And one of its major functions, I have hypothesized here, is a psychological one: to provide various "transitional solutions," various methods or mechanisms or techniques, shared by members of the culture, whose function is to *get persons out,* to sever the tie to the symbiotic mother. Cultural forms are created with the purpose of *assisting the individual in his struggle to separate.* Civilization or culture, from this point of view, may be viewed as a pattern or structure of ideas, modes of behavior, etc., whose function is to *assist the individual in his struggle for separation-individuation;* to structure the *struggle against regression* to the symbiotic object; and to provide various "sublimations," substitutes for the symbiotic dream in the external world which serve to make life (in the absence of the symbiotic bond) bearable.

Chapter IX

Culture as a Transitional Object

M. D. Faber, in his important book *Culture and Consciousness,* has put forth a theory similar to the one put forth here (1981). Faber argues that the early, traumatic separation from the mother is neither accepted nor mastered by the child. Rather, at the precise moment of the perception of separateness from the mother, the child *transfers* the attachment to the mother-complex onto other objects, transitional objects, which symbolize the mother complex:

> What serves the child magically as a "transitional object," as a method of retaining the tie to the parental figure during the time of separation is a symbol, an external "thing" that in the "cultural space" of the child's inner world corresponds to the internalized presence of the parent and becomes the "surrogate."
> (1981, p. 64)

> Religion is a transitional phenomenon, a transitional activity designed to accomplish precisely the end accomplished by the transitional object earlier described, the object which "gives" the child to the universe of culture and symbol at the same time that it "takes" the child away from the universe of the mother, the object which magically allows separation and reunion in the same psychological moment.
> (1981, p. 115)

According to Faber, the external "thing" in the cultural world corresponds to the "internalized presence of the parent" and becomes its "surrogate." In short, the cultural object is an *extrajected equivalent of the internalized object;* it is a way of perpetuating the tie to the infantile love-object by attaching to an *external object* rather than by internalizing the object.

This perspective suggests the possibility of a change in psychoanalytic theory which permits the *linkage* of this theory to the external, cultural world, thus increasing its power, and mending the "split" in psychoanalytic thought, the split which *separates* psychoanalysis from the responsibility to explore and explain "external reality" itself. That is to say: where the mechanism of internalization is viewed as the primary response to separation from the mother, psychoanalysis remains within the domain of the study of inner psychic structure. However, if we maintain, with Faber, that objects in cultural reality become *substitutes* for elements of inner psychic structure, *then the entire realm of culture comes under the purview or aegis of psychoanalytic thought.* We begin to explore the *contours and shape of cultural objects as they reflect inner psychic structure,* the way in which these objects shape, at the same time that they provide a definition for, our infantile fantasies.

When Faber views religion (a particular form of culture) as a "transitional activity" which "gives the child to the universe of culture and symbol at the same time that it takes the child away from the universe of the mother," when he views the transitional object as one which "magically allows separation and reunion in the same psychological moment," he is suggesting, as we have above, that the culture object functions to permit the *transference of libido,* functions to "move the individual along" from one phase of development to the next. *The regressive attachment serves as a progressive force,* insofar as the transference of energy from infantile objects onto other objects is what *causes these external objects to be invested with energy and interest.* It is the "magic" of the omnipotent bond to the mother which, when displaced onto cultural objects, gives them a "magical" quality, a quality which fascinates and intrigues us. Cultural objects have the quality of a phallic mother, a "fetishistic" quality.

According to Faber, what binds the individual to his culture, what ties the human being to the institutions of society, is precisely this projection of the infantile situation. The "bind" which we experience in relationship to culture is a replication of the earlier, infantile bind:

> The individual's struggle to establish and maintain "dual-unity" binds him to the objects of his inner world and, hence, to an overestimation of external objects that "automatically" become projective exemplifications of either acceptance or rejection; in other words, psychological symbols.
> (1981, p. 171)

> People are tied to the "institutions" of their "society" out of the tie that binds them to the parental figures within. The projection of internalized affect into the symbols of security and control, or more properly, the *epiphenomenal eliciting of internalized affect by the existing symbols of cultural life,* is an energic event.
> (1981, p. 200)

> The tie to society, the "social aspect," is ultimately rooted *zu liebe,* in the internalization, identification, and object relation, that commences during the early period and is subsequently projected onto the "social" landscape.
> (1981, p. 236)

The human connection to the social world, then, is fueled by the attachment to inner objects; the institutions of society attain their power and hold upon individuals because they serve as containers for the infantile energies and affects. The objects of culture become symbols of inner objects, and *because they do so* we idealize and become attached to these objects. The attachment to society is an "energic" event, and the energy which sustains the attachment to cultural objects is energy derived from the internal objects, which continue to exert their power upon the individual. Viewed more positively, we may suggest that the cultural objects serve as "releasers" for the energy which was previously "bound" in relationship to the internal objects. By virtue of their capacity to act as *symbols* of the inner objects, the individual is willing to abandon the attachment to the inner objects. Or, more precisely, the symbiotic fantasy of connectedness is not abandoned, but only *transferred* onto new objects, which serve to replicate the infantile experience of connectedness. The human being attaches himself to the omnipotent culture (and expects to be gratified by it) just as he once was attached to (and was gratified by) the omnipotent mother.

More generally, we may speculate, the attachment to the "world" becomes a substitute for the attachment to the mother. The world is experienced, not as an "external reality," but as a transitional object. The world becomes a symbol of the *other half of the self,* a symbol of the mother in the symbiotic fantasy. So that when one speaks of the "duality" of self and world, one is not necessarily speaking of a separate self or subject who perceives a separate world "out there" as an external reality. Rather, we may suggest, for many persons, the world, as an object of perception, is conceived as a *symbol of the symbiotic half of the self;* ultimately, as an extension of one's own body.

Chapter X

The Bodily Roots of the Symbol

If, as Faber has hypothesized, the attachment to culture inherits the attachment to the mother, then it follows that, in some way, the attachment of the individual to culture links his *body* to culture (or to the idea of culture). Thus, when Faber describes the attachment to culture as an "energic" tie, he is suggesting that it is *bodily energies* (libido) which fuel the attachment to culture. (The initial statement of this idea is the psychoanalytic idea that cultural forms are created on the basis of the *sublimation* of instinctual energies.)

We begin our analysis by emphasizing that, according to psychoanalysis, the fundamental source of human identity is the body. Thus, Freud's famous statement that

> the ego is first and foremost a bodily-ego; it is not merely a surface entity, but it is itself the projection of a surface.
> (1962, p. 26)

Similar, Deutsch states:

> The body represents to an individual the very reality which he cannot deny because to do so he would have to deny his existence. A new born child knows only one reality, i.e., his body which he can feel, touch, and perceive with his senses.
> (1959, p. 75)

Edward, et al., similarly stress the bodily origins of identity. Unlike Freud, however, they emphasize the source of the self as emanating from proprioceptive stimulation from *within* the body rather than stimulation from the *surface* of the body:

> Inner stimuli are experienced by proprioceptors such as the muscles, subcutaneous tissues, tendons, and joints, and by enteroceptors that receive sensations emanating from the stomach and the intestines. Over time, these are recorded in the mind and lead to a beginning awareness or cathexis of the inside of the body. These early inner body experiences contribute, ultimately, to the development of the body-ego and the body-self, forming the very core of the self.
>
> (1981, p. 5)

Whether one focuses upon the *ego* as emanating from surface stimulation, or upon the *self* as derived from internal stimulation, it is clear that, from a psychoanalytic point of view, the root of the sense of self is the concrete experience of one's own body.

We have observed that the child, during the symbiotic phase of development, imagines the mother to be a part of himself, an extension of his own body. We have also noted that, in his denial of separateness, the child *internalizes* the mother. Consequently, as Brown emphasizes, the human ego consists of a duality, the "dual unity" of child and mother.

If the ego is a body-ego, and the ego is also *dual* in nature, consisting of the child's perception of his own body plus his experience of the mother's body as an extension of his own body, it follows that *the body ego is dual as well.* The body ego constitutes both the experience of one's own body and the *experience of one's mother as she ministers to one's body.* As the term "symbiosis" implies, it is the experience of a *dual-body* which is the source of the human ego.

Later, when internalization occurs, the fantasy of another object (another *body*) contained within the structure of the ego is perpetuated. Psychoanalysis has traditionally conceived of this change as the development of a new "psychic structure," which has been called the super-ego, the internalized object, etc. What we have stressed in this monograph is that this "encapsulation" of the mother within the self, as an internalized object, *continues to exert a profound influence upon the body.* The "mental representation" of the mother is a mental representation of *the mother's body;* the body-ego which contained the "symbiotic half of the self" is perpetuated in the internal psychic structure. The super-ego, in short, is a *psychosomatic entity.* Faber puts this idea forth with clarity:

> The "object" of the inward realm is in a very real sense intangible, immeasurable, invisible, a kind of information "trace" in the "mental apparatus." Yet it is rooted in the body, in the senses; it is connected inextricably to the physical organism. It cannot be addressed, or touched, or altered, apart from the tissues in which it lives. To a significant degree, it is the perceiving body through which it governs the human being's sensorial feedback system.
> (1985, p. 168)

The development of the *symbol,* or symbolic object (such as the nation) occurs later, and its function is to *represent the lost mother or the symbiotic part of the self from which one has been separated.* The object serves to "re-connect" the individual with the lost part of the self, but now through the mechanism of attachment to an object which symbolizes the lost part of the self. This "transitional object" serves to link the individual with the world, where once he had been attached to his mother.

Put somewhat differently: The mother, in the symbiotic situation, is "coenesthetically experienced as a part of the self." Separation from the mother, therefore, is separation from the "omnipotent body of childhood," separation from the "dual unity." This experience of the diminution of the self, of the mutilation of the self, of the loss of omnipotence and sense of "smallness," leads to the effort to *reconnect with another omnipotent object.* This re-connection often takes the form of an attachment to a *symbol* which represents the omnipotent mother. The symbol, therefore, may be viewed as the *container for the lost part of the self,* the form in which the omnipotent mother is "embodied." We have hypothesized that, in contemporary cultures, the "nation" functions as a *shared symbolic system.* And that this shared symbol, the nation, is a *symbol of the omnipotent mother,* a substitute for the symbiotic part of the self. This "omnipotent body," the nation, is a substitute for the mother's body. Now, the individual "re-connects" with his lost omnipotence by attaching himself to the omnipotent nation.

The process we are describing here, as noted earlier, has much in common with the *conversion process.* Let us recapitulate our previous discussion and expand upon it. According to Deutsch:

> The child soon discovers that what he once felt as part of himself is temporarily or permanently lost. This first awareness of a loss is the origin of a fantasy or illusion, because what is no longer in the realm of, or attached to, the body has disappeared and now belongs to another reality, so to speak. The child reacts to this loss of an object with the attempt to regain it, to retrieve this part of himself, by imagining it. Attempts of this nature continue throughout life and can be considered as the origin of the conversion process.
> (1959, pp. 75-76)

Rephrased in terms of the theory of symbiosis: When the child begins to perceive that the symbiotic mother is not a part of himself, that she exists as a separate object in external reality, he attempts to *negate* this perception by creating a fantasy or illusion, the purpose of which is to "retrieve the lost part of the self." This fantasy attaches to *bodily parts:*

> The feeling of object loss [is] a ferment for the symbolization process...each part of the body possesses the potentiality for the symbolic expression of loss and separation. This loss evokes anxiety which, as Freud stated, is a separation anxiety. Hence it calls for replacement. A more highly developed ego turns to different parts of the body which are adequately symbolized and may serve as substitutes for the loss.
> (1959, p. 79)

Thus, the lost other is internalized into the body, and is symbolized *within specific bodily parts.* The "conversion symptom," from this point of view, may be described as the *possession of a bodily part by the internalized other.* Because the bodily part is "identified" with an object, it loses its capacity to function in a natural, organic way. The body is "possessed" by the internalized other, which acts as a "weight of oppression." The body loses its motility and flexibility as a result of the fact that it is being used as a "container for the lost other."

Psychoanalytic thinkers have stressed the *bodily* sources of symbolism. Thus, for example, Deutsch states:

> The memory symbols have thus developed from a specific sensory perception of one's own body, which has been projected onto the external object.
> (1959, p. 76)

According to Rycroft:

> Symbols may arise in a last resort from bodily perceptions which are common to all mankind.
> (quoted in Deutsch, 1959, p. 78)

And Kubie (1953) hypothesizes that:

> the autogeny of all symbolic processes has some of its roots in our evolving percepts and concepts of the body.
> (quoted in Deutsch, 1959, p. 79)

In terms of the present theory we may modify this conception as follows: The symbol in the external world represents a projection of the *body part in which the internalized object is contained*. The symbol symbolizes *both* the bodily part which has been transformed or modified by the internal object, and the object contained within that bodily part. The symbol is a projection, in short, of the dual-unity itself, a projection of mother-contained-within-body.

One of the psychological functions of this projective mechanism, therefore, would appear to be the attempt to *liberate* a specific bodily part by *externalizing the object which is contained within it*. The effort is made to *distance* the internalized object from the self, from one's actual body, by externalizing it into an object which seems to exist at a distance from the body. As Deutsch states:

> If no surrogate object is available, conversion symptoms are formed. This can lead to partial or complete inhibition or to hyperactivity of a bodily function.
> (1959, p. 77)

In short, if one is unable to project the psychic complex away from the body into a surrogate object, then a conversion symptom is formed, which means that the other contained within the self leads to the "inhibition or hyperactivity of a body function." The bodily part is *sexualized* because the body part functions to mediate a "relationship" between the self and the object, a relationship between the self and the object which is now contained *precisely within the fabric of one's own body*. For example, the symbiotic mother may be projected into the *right arm* (the mother becomes one's "right hand man"). One is inhibited in doing things for oneself because one is dependent upon the internalized object, which is "contained" within one's right arm. One expects the right arm to function magically or automatically, "mother will do it"; the functioning of the will is inhibited by the passive attachment to the internalized object, which exists within a bodily organ. The arm is both "self" and it is a container for the object. The "self-object" is merged within the musculature of one's body. One's arm becomes lazy and dependent ("let mama do it").

With symbolization, with the development of the transitional object, the internalized object is *externalized,* thus separating it from the body and freeing the body part in which the object was contained. The dependent attachment to the internalized object existing within one's own body is transformed into a dependent attachment upon an object which symbolizes the bodily-part-plus-object-contained-within-body-part. Symbolism, from this point of view, is a defense against the conversion symptom, a way of liberating the body by separating (distancing) the internal object from the core of the self.

The mechanism of symbolism, then, is a mechanism which involves the projection of an intrapsychic perception of the body into the external world, into various objects in the world which *symbolize* the body. The burden of being fused with an internal object, the burden of having an object so close to one's body, is lifted through the externalization of the internal object; the object in the external world is an object which symbolizes the internal object. The individual continues to connect with, to attach to, the object. But now he connects to an object "out there," an object which seems to exist within social reality. There is a *distancing* of the object from the self, and thus it can be "perceived," and managed more easily.

We may hypothesize an additional consequence of this projective mechanism: Once symbolization occurs, once the body is projected into an external object, then *the body or self comes to be "contained" in the external object;* a part of the self has been projected "out there," so that the body or self now exists in the form of an external object which symbolizes the body or self. In attempting to *liberate* the body or self, the individual *loses* himself. The human being no longer contains himself, he no longer exists within himself; now he exists in objects outside the self. He exists as a symbol of himself.

In other words, the external object contains the projected part of the self. The individual's ego has been split into two. Now the "other half of the self" (the symbiotic mother), previously internalized, has been externalized. The self-object has been split into two, the ego becomes a duality, and *part of the self exists in the form of a symbol into which the self has been projected.* The individual identifies himself with these "surrogate objects," such as the nation, objects which come to stand for the self. The body has been placed for "safe-keeping" in an external object, which now contains and "preserves" the object. One *identifies* with the object (e.g., the nation) into which one's self has been projected.

It follows logically that once the body has been externalized into an object which symbolizes the body, the individual will find it necessary to re-internalize the symbolic object as a way of recovering the wholeness of his body, as a way of reunifying the self. Deutsch defines this process of re-internalizing the symbiotic object as "retrojection" (re-introjection), and describes it as follows:

> [The] specific sensory stimulus...serves as the mediator for the retrojection of the lost object onto that organ system which is its symbolic representative.
>
> (1959, p. 76)

> The sense of reality originates from the projection of sensory perceptions of one's own body onto objects outside of it, since external objects are perceived as if severed from the body and lost. This separation leads to the continual wish to restore the loss of the bodily wholeness. The objects outside become reunited with the body by way of symbolization. I propose to call this process "retrojection." The physiologic function of those body parts which have become the representatives of these symbolized objects are for this reason modified on account of the process of symbolic action.
>
> (1959, p. 76)

> I consider symbolization as one of the most important factors which are immanent in the conversion process and which alter the physiologic processes from the beginning of life. It fuses together the body parts which as symbolic representations have become separated and can only become reunited by being given symbolic meaning.
>
> (1959, p. 78)

Retrojection, therefore, functions to "reunite outside objects with the body," functions to "fuse together the body parts which have become separated." As a consequence of the retrojection of the symbolic object, "the physiologic function of those body parts which have become the representatives of the symbolized objects are modified." In other words, in a sense we are "back where we started from."

In order to recover the unity of the body, the wholeness of the body, which was lost because the body was projected into objects outside the self, it is now necessary to retroject back into the body the *symbols* of the body which contain the projected body. Thus, for example, the individual "identifies with the nation." That object which had served as the container for the internalized object, which represented a projection of the symbiotic mother, must now be retrojected back into the self. The Nazis, for example, commonly made statements such as the following: "Hitler is Germany, just as Germany is Hitler." Thus, by virtue of this mechanism, the primary identification with the mother is restored. The dual-unity of self-mother is restored by an equation which makes "self-country" a singular entity. The lost part of the self has been "recaptured" through the mechanism of an *absolute identification* whereby the object in the external world which *symbolizes* the lost self has come to be identified with the self. In thus retrojecting the symbolic object (the nation) back into the self, the unity of the self is restored.

Put another way: In separating from his actual mother, Hitler identifies with the German nation, which serves as a symbolic substitute for the lost object. As a lost, wandering youth, with no anchor in reality, he projects his existence into Germany which, however, is perceived to exist at great distance from himself. He has "split" his ego into two, the concrete person, Adolf Hitler, and that part of himself which exists in the form of a projection, that part of himself which "identifies" with Germany. The "self-object" has been split into Hitler-Germany. His "soul" has been externalized.

Hitler seeks to attain power, therefore, as a way of *consolidating* the identification between himself and Germany, as a way of *getting closer* to the projective object (which contains his self). He seeks to attain power as a way of *recapturing the lost part of himself.* When he becomes Fuehrer of the German nation he can finally say: "Hitler is Germany. Germany is Hitler." Now he has *recovered,* so to speak, the lost part of himself, by creating an *absolute identity* between himself and the object which contains the lost part of the self. He has now, in this symbolic form, "restored his body wholeness" by completely *retrojecting* the symbolic object into the self.

Now, however, in spite of the fact that he has "fulfilled his wish," he is confronted with the fundamental dilemma all over again: the danger of *fusion,* the danger of merging with, and being overwhelmed by, the omnipotent object. Now Hitler is *possessed* by the object, he is possessed by Germany. *Germany exists within the very fiber of his physiology,* just as the symbiotic mother once did. Consequently, in my view, Hitler then must act in such a manner as to *destroy the object with which he imagines himself to be fused.* The destruction of Germany, for Hitler, has the purpose of a struggle to *liberate himself from the object which possesses him,* to liberate himself from Germany. He imagines himself to be *connected to,* to be fused with, this massive, omnipotent object; to manage the entire German nation is a tremendous *burden.* To liberate himself, therefore, is to destroy the object which oppresses him, the object with which he identifies, Germany. By this time, however, the identification is so complete that Hitler must *destroy himself* in order to destroy Germany.

We may summarize the process we have been describing here as follows: (1) The perception of the loss of the object or part of the self leads to the development of an illusion, or fantasy, whose purpose is to retrieve the lost part of the self, by imagining it. (2) In the conversion process, the fantasy of the lost object is projected into specific bodily parts, so that one's own body comes to contain or symbolize the lost object. (3) Symbolization is the mechanism whereby sensory perceptions in one's own body are projected into objects outside the body. (4) One of the purposes of symbolism is to "liberate" the bodily part, to free it from the conversion symptom by *externalizing* the part of the body which contains the internalized object. This mechanism serves to distance the object from the self, and so to relieve the individual of some of the anxiety associated with the fusion fantasy. (5) Insofar as a part of the self now exists in a symbol, which is perceived as external to the self, retrojection of the object must then occur in the form of the introjection of the symbolic object. (6) Retrojection of the symbolic object functions to restore the loss of the body's wholeness, to "fuse together the body" which had become "torn apart" when the body was projected into the symbolic object. Identification with the symbol (e.g., the nation) is the mechanism whereby the individual *re-unites with the lost parts of the self*.

Deutsch's summary of the process is as follows:

> Only when the fantasy and dream world are embedded in the reality of the body does the process of symbolization begin. Previous to that, however, the body or body parts of the lost object are searched for in one's own body....The body ego owes its development to a great extent to the incorporation of another one into itself. The process of symbolization originates

in the need to make good for the loss of the body's integrity by reintegrating into it adequate substitutes. The symbolization substitutes the amount of loss which the lost object represented to the individual.

(1959, p. 80)

Of crucial significance for understanding the process of nationalism is the statement that "symbolization substitutes the amount of loss which the lost object represented to the individual." If we are correct in viewing the nation as a projection of the symbiotic mother from which one has been separated, then the fact that the symbolic object, the nation, must be such a *big, massive object* testifies to the *intensity or quantity of the loss* which is experienced by the child upon his perception of separation from the mother. The early identification with the mother constituted a *big part of the self.* The child existed *only in relationship to the mother,* and he conceived of the object in omnipotent terms. Consequently, when he perceives that he is a small, frail, separate being, the loss is so severe, the blow to his ego so traumatic, that he can only compensate for this separation by imagining that he is *still attached to something big, glorious, powerful, omnipotent.* Only something as grandiose as an *entire nation* will serve to compensate him for his loss. His ego must be "blown up," projected into this massive, omnipotent object. Hitler is not content to be a solitary individual. He must equate his ego with the *entire German nation.* But, in this regard, he is not unusual. For, if the theory presented in this monograph is correct, *every human being* compensates for the early loss, a loss which is conceived to be an enormous one, by *attaching himself to his country or "culture" as a symbolic object which can symbolize, or substitute for the lost part of the self,* which can serve as a substitute for the omnipotent, symbiotic mother from which one has been forced to separate.

We have been focusing, in this section, on the bodily roots of the symbol. But it is clear that there is a profound *transformation* which occurs as a result of symbolization, a profound change in psychic structure. It is not our task, here, to examine the details of this psychic change. We have hypothesized, however, that the transformation of libido attached to the body into libido attached to symbolic objects has a particular psychic function, and that that function is to *get the child away,* to free the child from his mother's body, and to connect him with objects in the external world which constitute the pathway toward social reality. The symbol is a "linking object" which gets the child away from the mother; it is a "way station," both a point of departure and a new reality. That is: The symbolic object can become a new reality only because it can symbolize the point of departure.

One of the crucial dimensions of the symbol, of course, is that it possesses *an abstract or intellectual quality*. While the nation, for example, may, on the unconscious level, represent an actual human body, it is clear that the process of symbolization creates an entirely new dimension of reality. The path toward the symbol, toward projection, toward externalization, toward culture and civilization, is the path toward the *desexualization* of the early bodily, libidinal attachments. Sexual energy is used to create something new; the attachment to one's own body and to the body of one's mother is sequestered for the creation of cultural reality. Presumably, as libido gathers around the idea or symbol, the symbol becomes desexualized or "de-bodified," cut off from the source in the body, from which it initially derived.

But at the crux of psychoanalytic thinking has always been the tendency to be skeptical of modes of thought which "de-link" man's cognitive, intellectual development from his physiology. So that while we can agree that the symbolic process is the source of a tremendous transformation, we must still wonder about the extent to which a "split" between the symbol and its bodily source occurs. Does the symbol "drain the libido away," cutting it off from its source in the body? Or, beneath the attachment to culture, may we still perceive *bodily energies and bodily fantasies* which fuel this attachment? If we agree that the human being, as part of the animal kingdom, can never separate himself from his body and bodily energies, then we must define, in a more precise way, *the nature of the transformation* which occurs when bodily energies are changed into energies used in relationship to symbols.

Chapter XI

The Bodily Roots of Culture

What is emphasized in the work of M. D. Faber is that the symbol never loses its connection with the body. And that, therefore, all of the conflict and ambivalence surrounding the fantasy of merger and the struggle for separation-individuation are "inherited" in the individual's relationships with the objects which symbolize the infantile objects. He states:

> Mental contents cannot be separated from bodily contents....The symbol, with its space and time, is rooted in the body, grows out of the body, is but a "higher" development of body awareness.
>
> (1981, p. 97)

> Internalization is not simply a psychological but a psycho-physical process. The infant and young child who takes in the object experiences that object in his body, in his anxious respiration, in his posture of avoidance, in his stiff, contracted frustration and rage. The splitting and divisiveness of the early time transpire within the cells of the organism, only later to be "raised" to the level of symbolic representation. But even when anxiety, tension and divisiveness are "raised" to the symbolic level, they retain their hold upon the body; they still exist, as persistently and as powerfully as ever, in the individual's "length of blood and bone."
>
> (1981, p. 97)

Faber emphasizes, as we have, the *physiological* consequences of internalization, suggesting that the early conflicts surrounding separation-individuation continue to "transpire within the cells of the organism." He argues, further, that the conflict surrounding this phase of development does not disappear when it is "raised to the level of symbolic representation." In other words, we may suggest, the fundamental conflicts which we have outlined, the conflict between the wish to individuate versus the wish to regress, the wish to merge versus the fear of merger, etc., are "played out" in relationship to the symbolic objects which represent the infantile objects.

Thus, the "discontent" which is elicited by civilization, the experience of society as *oppressive*, may grow out of the *ambivalence toward culture as a symbolic object*. The individual tends to become *dependently attached* to the objects of culture, to link himself in a powerful way to the society in which he exists, to *fuse* his personal identity with the objects of culture, just as he had symbiotically bound himself to his mother. In short, the infantile, symbiotic tie to the mother is *transferred* onto the idea of one's culture and to objects in culture, and one comes to feel "bound up" with these ideas and objects. *Culture becomes an omnipotent extension of the self,* the "other half" of the self in the symbiotic situation, and the individual feels "connected" to this omnipotent body.

The *struggle for separation and individuality, therefore, may come to be played out in relationship to one's society.* The culture may become like an omnipotent mother, pervading one's consciousness, creating the *fear of merger or fusion with the culture.* Culture may come to approximate the power of the internalized object for the psychotic, and threaten to cause the "loss of self."

More likely, however, the individual will embrace his *identification* with the objects of culture, fusing his identity with these objects, much as he did in the symbiotic phase. It is as if one possesses an unselfconscious, innocent *belief* (reflecting one's experience during the symbiotic phase) that there is a powerful object existing "out there" in the world; that one exists in a state of connectedness to this object; and that if one can intensify and consolidate this connection, gratification, security and power will be assured.

At the same time, as one "takes in" more and more of one's culture (a displaced introjection of the omnipotent mother), the projected object (culture) may come to be experienced as an oppressive burden, as an "encrustation" which grows around the self. What can occur is that *the individual can come to be "possessed" by the society just as he once was possessed by the mother.*

Faber emphasizes that it is the *link* between the *inner psychic realm* and the external cultural realm which is the source of the *power* which we attribute to the external cultural realm, as well as of the experience of being "dominated" by the cultural realm:

> The power that binds the individual to culture, that stands behind all social and religious phenomena, is ultimately drawn from the inner world, from the individual's psycho-physical connection to the internalized objects of infancy and childhood.
> (1981, p. 148)

> The initial and primal "domination" of human experience is the "domination" of the individual by the objects within--the "immortal objects" whose persistent, implacable influence stands squarely behind those forms of "domination" that eventually characterize the social world.
> (1981, p. 207)

Insofar as the individual's relationship to the internalized object is a "psycho-physical" one, then the individual's relationship to objects which exist as projections of internalized objects is psycho-physical as well: The individual is psychosomatically bound to his culture. Insofar as he cathects the objects of his culture, and insofar as these objects symbolize the internalized object, then *the entire complex of emotions and attitudes experienced in relationship to the internal objects may then exist in relationship to the objects of culture.*

For example, if one "loves" one's nation, this is because the nation is an object which symbolizes one's mother. The nation is the cultural object which contains the "transference neurosis." If a man is willing to "sacrifice his life" for the nation, this is because he *cannot bear to be separated from the symbiotic mother,* and will perform any act in the name of maintaining the delusion of her protective omnipotence. The "ideals" of the individual, in short, are the *projection of narcissistic libido onto the various ideas and objects which constitute "culture".* (And thus any individual who is attached to a cultural object will find the "interpretation" of this attachment quite unpleasant, for the following reason: His very selfhood has become identified with the cultural object, his very *soul* has become identified with an "ideal" which now exists, not within him, but as an object in the "external world." To deprive him of his belief in the omnipotence of the object with which he identifies, therefore, is to deprive him of the ground of his being, to separate him from himself. To deprive him of his cultural ideals is to separate him from the object which contains his soul.)

In a similar way, the experience of the *dominating quality* of culture is rooted in the experience of the *dominating quality of the internal object.* Just as one cannot "escape" the object on the inside, so does one come to feel that one cannot escape one's "culture" on the outside. The experience of being "crowded," as the internalized object impinges upon the self, is replicated in the experience of the oppressive, burdensome quality of one's involvement with society. The "self-object" becomes "self-society," and one feels the same claustrophobic attachment, the same sense that one's culture is "all around one" and is inescapable. The culture becomes like an omnipotent breast (e.g., the American supermarket), with the same sense of paralysis and helplessness which arose from the experience of fusion with an internalized object.

Sociologists tend to view society as a "real entity" which can control the behavior and thought-patterns of individuals. The idea that "culture determines behavior" has a mystical aspect to it, as if culture is some abstract "force" which hovers above the individual, and directs him to behave in various ways, like an unseen puppet-master. If we adopt Faber's conceptualization, however, the psychic meaning of the phrase "culture determines behavior" becomes clearer. What seems to be occurring is that the individual *attaches to his culture as a symbolic object;* he invests libidinal energy in the *idea* of his own society. This attachment is rooted, in turn, in his tendency to *project the internalized object onto the objects of culture.* It is this *projection of the internal bond which gives the idea of society its power.* The culture is experienced as an enormous "national body" with which one's own body is fused. And it is precisely the identification of one's culture with an omnipotent body which causes us to idealize its patterns of thinking and behavior. We follow the patterns because "obeying" seems to promise omnipotence. To "do as mother tells us" is to share in her omnipotence, is to be bound together with millions of others within the fabric of this gigantic "body."

Through this mechanism, society *gets control over our bodies*. The "self-object" becomes "self-in-society," and the paralyzing dependency toward the symbiotic mother is "replicated" on this "higher level." In the most extreme case, one is willing to "sacrifice one's life for the nation." Millions of Germans, millions of Japanese, bound in a symbiotic tie to the projection of the omnipotent mother ("Germany," "Japan") run to their deaths in their refusal to separate from the omnipotent object. Death in war, then, becomes "re-fusion" with the nation: the restoration of the unconscious symbiotic tie, the restoration of "oneness," the fusion of self and nation.

Chapter XII

Repression

"Repression" was initially viewed by Freud as an unconscious process whereby the ego, often at the behest of the super-ego, prevented libidinal ideas and libidinal energies from entering into consciousness. Repression was conceived as an *unconscious psychic mechanism,* the end result being that the organism was denied access to its own libidinal energies. Insofar as the individual did not have access to his libidinal energy, he was denied both the pleasure of sexual gratification and the capacity to use his psychic energy (derived from the libido) for the task of transforming reality. Repression, as a psychic mechanism, caused the libidinal energies to become "stuck within." The cure of neurosis, from this perspective, was connected to the overcoming of repression: the "bound" libidinal energies, sustained by the repressive "counter-cathexes," were to be made available to consciousness.

From the very beginning, of course, Freud linked the repressive forces within the individual to the "repressive society." The hypothesized connection between culture and repression culminated in *Civilization and Its Discontents* (1962). Norman O. Brown continued in this tradition, exploring the sources of repression and neurosis in human culture. It is in M. D. Faber's work, however, that we begin to perceive, in a more precise way, the manner in which the psychic force of repression links up with cultural forces. Faber states:

> The underlying significance of Freud's suggestion that repression and guilt constitute the cornerstone of "civilization" is apparent. Repression allows the body to remain in its converted condition, tied to the object, doomed to discontent,

and taken over by *the institutional forces of civilization that derive their power through a psycho-physical extension of the parental bond.*

(1981, p. 102)

In short, according to Faber, it is the *tie to the internalized object* which is the source of repression. Repression becomes linked to "society" insofar as the *body is taken over by the institutional forces of civilization through a psycho-physical extension of the parental bond.* It is because *the attachment to civilization inherits the attachment to the internalized object* that civilization comes to represent a "repressive force." The libidinal energies of the individual become "sequestered" for use by civilization when *civilization symbolizes the internalized object to which one is attached.* The "super-ego" is not merely a "psychic structure." It is a love-object. And it is the *projection of the attachment to this love-object onto the idea of civilization* which is the source of the power which civilization exerts upon us, and our willingness to abandon our own gratifications and interests in the name of "serving" this "love-object." (I do not wish to discuss this idea in detail here, but I believe it was the *sexual revolution* of the 1970s--itself strongly influenced by psychoanalytic thinkers such as Freud and Brown--which permitted this internal connection to be perceived more clearly. That is to say: the sexual revolution involved the breaking down of the super-ego as a "structure" or "frozen introject." What was revealed was a *libidinally cathected internal object.*)

We have noted that the infantile love-object, the mother, becomes internalized, so that the child's relationship to the omnipotent, symbiotic mother is preserved in his relationship to the internalized object. Repression, from this point of view, may be conceptualized in terms of a relationship with the internalized object. Specifically, the fact that libido is not available for use in sexual relationships or for the transformation of reality is due to the fact that this libido is *bound up in a relationship with an internalized object.* The libido, one may hypothesize, is used to *sustain the life of the internalized object,* that is, to sustain the fantasy of fusion with the omnipotent mother. The libidinal energy is used to *sustain the delusion of the symbiotic tie,* now experienced in the form of a tie to an inner object, an inner "companion." Repression, then, is this internalized "relationship" with the love-object, the use of psychic energy in the *inward realm.*

"Repression," according to this theory, is actually a case of the *involution of libido:* The individual's psychic energy is being used to *sustain his relationship with an internalized object.* He has to provide psychic fuel in order to "keep the object alive." Thus, what once was a symbiotic tie in which the child was the recipient of energy, a tie in which the child passively *received* energy through the activity of the mother, now becomes reversed: *the internalized object becomes symbiotic upon the self.* The individual must "feed the object;" must feed it with his own libido and psychic energy in order to "keep it alive," to sustain its "presence" within. Since this inner object is conceived as an *omnipotent object,* since it is conceived to be enormously powerful, it takes a *great deal of energy to keep the fantasy alive,* to maintain the life of this inner "companion." Libidinal energy is "drained off" into the realm of fantasy, into the realm of the inner object, and is not available for use in reality.

When the omnipotent, internal object is displaced into the omnipotent nation, or onto one's omnipotent culture, the struggle to maintain the life of the object through the expenditure of libido is likewise displaced into this "outer realm." Now the monster within becomes the "monster" of one's omnipotent culture, and one must "feed it" with one's own energies in order to keep it alive. In order to preserve and sustain the "omnipotent body of culture" (analogous to a "humongous breast"), one must direct vast quantities of libido toward it.

It is at this point that the concept of *repression* merges with the concept of *sacrifice:* just as the individual sacrificed his own psychic energies in the name of maintaining the life of the internalized object (upon which he believed his own survival depended), so does he now sacrifice his energies in the name of sustaining his tie to the culture, or to his nation. All of this is in the name of sustaining a *dream of connection to an omnipotent object,* a fantasy which is a defense against the perception of separateness, loneliness, and death. It is a refusal to acknowledge the solitariness of the self. In fusing one's own ego with the gigantic "body of the nation" (a projection of the omnipotent, symbiotic half of the self), one experiences oneself to be more than one actually is.

If we return to Mahler's definition of the symbiotic phase, we will be able to perceive this process more clearly. Mahler defines symbiosis as "somatopsychic omnipotent fusion with the representation of the mother," as the "delusion of a common boundary of two actually and physically separate individuals," and as the phase in which the infant behaves and functions as though he and his mother were "an omnipotent system--a dual unity with one common boundary."

Libidinal energy which is bound up with the internalized object and later projected into the body of the nation, then, functions to *sustain the illusion that one is a dual system.* The "dual unity" of self-mother becomes the dual unity of "self-in-nation." We *sustain the illusion that we are a dual-system rather than a unity* by linking our personal identities to this "omnipotent object," the nation. The "boundary" of this system is the boundary of one's nation, and one exists "within the boundary of one's nation;" one is fused with the body of one's culture. The delusion of "somatopsychic omnipotent fusion with the (mental) representation of the mother" becomes the delusion of fusion with a symbolic projection of the mother, the nation. One exists in a *somatopsychic tie* with one's nation. The *blood* which is sacrificed in the name of the nation (whether in the name of "wars," or more directly, as in the case of Aztec civilization) is a paradigm for the sacrifice of one's life energies in the name of preserving the delusion of the omnipotence of this *symbolic object,* with which one is now "fused." When the totalitarian argues that there *does not exist a dimension of reality which is separate from the state,* when the Communist declares that individual life has meaning only as it contributes to the life of the "whole," he is replicating this delusion of an "omnipotent system," of a "dual unity." He is affirming that existence is not possible in separation from the symbiotic mother; and that, in fact, there is a *common boundary* which links the individual, which "contains him"--the boundary of the nation-state.

So it is not precise to state that "civilization causes repression," as if civilization were a force independent of the wishes and psychic structure of human beings. What occurs is that the individual needs to *attach* to civilization as a means of replicating the omnipotent, symbiotic bond. And it is *precisely this need for attachment* which is the motive for "sacrifice," the motive which causes him to "bleed for the country," to sacrifice his own energies in the name of preserving the idea of this omnipotent object.

We can thus understand the manner in which the individual's body can be taken over by civilization, the manner in which the libidinal energies of individuals can be "sequestered" for the "civilization project." It is not that "society" acts at a distance, controlling one's behavior as if through magic. Rather, it is an *inner fantasy* which connects the individual to society, a fantasy which is displaced onto the *idea* of society; and it is therefore the *fantasy of being connected to the symbolic object, society,* which motivates the individual to perform activities "in the name" of this object. The *fantasy* is the link between the body and the symbolic object. And, as we have seen, the fundamental fantasy which fuels the connection to society is the *symbiotic tie to the mother,* which is "replicated" as a tie to the body of the nation. The individual is held in thralldom to this giant "transitional object." The "giantess of the nursery" (Edmund Bergler) becomes the great and glorious country, and the infantile attachment is perpetuated.

In summary: Repression, as a psychic mechanism, is rooted in the tie to the internal object. Libidinal energy is used in sustaining a relationship with the inner object and, because it is thus "bound" within, is not available for use in relationship to external objects and reality. Libidinal energy is used, rather, to sustain the fantasy of the "second part of a dual system," an inner psychic system which seems to promise power, security, gratification.

The symbiotic tie to the mother is past history. But the individual attempts to perpetuate this tie by preserving the object within, hoping the inner object will continue to "feed" him. In reality, the time of feeding is over. So one feeds oneself with one's own fantasy. But it takes *psychic energy* to maintain this illusion of a second object within the self. The individual must "feed the dream" in order to keep it alive. Symbiosis becomes a *symbiosis in reverse.* The fantasy of a symbiotic, internal object becomes *parasitical* upon the individual's organismic functioning, draining his energies. And it is precisely this need to "feed the internal object," to maintain an *inner* relationship which, in my view, is at the root of the mechanism of "repression."

When the infantile, symbiotic object becomes projected into the country, or society, a similar mechanism is operative. Now, however, the energy which had been used to sustain the inner object is *transferred* onto the symbolic object, and the energy is used to *sustain the fantasy of an omnipotent object "in reality,"* and to sustain the delusion that one is *connected* to this object. Energies which had been bound within are now somewhat liberated, insofar as the energy can be transferred to an object which seems to exist as a part of the external world. The energy "reaches out" to become transformed into a devotion to one's nation, to one's society, to one's culture, etc. But this "third dimension" of reality, the dimension of the "public sphere," the dimension of the nation, is actually, still, an emanation of inner psychic functioning. The nation is a transitional object, a shared delusion which is created by the "members" of society, in complicity with one another. The "world" of the nation is neither subjective nor objective, neither self nor other. It is a world which exists in the "twilight zone," a world of projected fantasy, *a projection held in common by the members of society,* which serves to unite them.

Civilization causes "discontent," therefore, because it "syphons off" the energy of the individual. Energies which might be used for the betterment of one's self, for the improvement of one's personal life, is "deflected" into the culture, and is used to sustain the delusion of the existence of an omnipotent object somewhere "out there," an omnipotent object with which the individual tries frantically to "connect," but which remains distant, abstract, inaccessible. The discontent, therefore, is *precisely the attachment to civilization:* on the one hand the enormous quantities of libido which are used in order to sustain this attachment; and on the other the *disillusionment* which occurs when the individual realizes that he can never really connect with this object. Unlike the symbiotic mother, who provided real bodily contact, real gratification, real pleasure, the gratifications of "national life" are so distant, so abstract. However abundant the "offerings" of the culture, however relentless the flow of information, entertainment, products, etc., society, as Geza Roheim once said, can never provide the gratification of a "good breast." In the *struggle,* however, to maintain contact with this omnipotent object, the life of the individual, the life of the self, is severely diminished.

References

Brown, N. O. (1959). *Life Against Death: The Psychoanalytic Meaning of History*. Middletown, Conn.: Wesleyan University Press.

Brown, N. O. (1966). *Love's Body*. New York: Vintage Books.

Deutsch, F. (1959). Symbolization as a Formative Stage of the Conversion Process. In F. Deutsch, ed., *On the Mysterious Leap from the Mind to the Body: A Study on the Theory of Conversion*. New York: International Universities Press.

Edward, J., N. Ruskin and P. Turrini (1981). *Separation-Individuation: Theory and Application*. New York: Gardner Press.

Faber, M. D. (1981). *Culture and Consciousness: The Social Meaning of Altered Awareness*. New York: Human Science Press.

Faber, M. D. (1985). *Objectivity and Human Perception*. Edmonton, Canada: The University of Alberta Press.

Freud, S. (1962). *The Ego and the Id*. New York: W. W. Norton.

Frosch, John (1983). *The Psychotic Process*. New York: International Universities Press.

Horton, P. C. (1981). *Solace: The Missing Dimension in Psychiatry*. Chicago: University of Chicago Press.

Kaplan, L. (1978). *Oneness and Separateness*. New York: Simon and Schuster.

Koenigsberg, R. A. (1975). *Hitler's Ideology: A Study in Psychoanalytic Sociology*. New York: The Library of Social Science.

Koenigsberg, R. A. (1977). *The Psychoanalysis of Racism, Revolution and Nationalism*. New York: The Library of Social Science.

Mahler, M. S. and M. Furer (1968). *On Human Symbiosis and the Vicissitudes of Individuation*. New York: International Universities Press.

Modell, A. H. (1968). *Object Love and Reality*. New York: International Universities Press.